IMAGES OF W

CW00370122

LUFTWAFFE BOMBERS IN THE BATTLE OF BRITAIN

RARE PHOTOGRAPHS FROM WARTIME ARCHIVES

Andy Saunders

Pen & Sword
AVIATION

First published in Great Britain in 2014 by
PEN & SWORD AVIATION
An imprint of
Pen & Sword Books Ltd
47 Church Street
Barnsley
South Yorkshire
S70 2AS

ISBN 978-1-78303-024-8

Typeset by Concept, Huddersfield, West Yorkshire HD4 5JL.
Printed and bound in England by CPI Group (UK) Ltd, Croydon CR0 4YY.

Pen & Sword Books Ltd incorporates the imprints of Pen & Sword Archaeology, Atlas, Aviation, Battleground, Discovery, Family History, History, Maritime, Military, Naval, Politics, Railways, Select, Social History, Transport, True Crime, and Claymore Press, Frontline Books, Leo Cooper, Praetorian Press, Remember When, Seaforth Publishing and Wharncliffe.

For a complete list of Pen & Sword titles please contact
PEN & SWORD BOOKS LIMITED
47 Church Street, Barnsley, South Yorkshire, S70 2AS, England
E-mail: enquiries@pen-and-sword.co.uk
Website: www.pen-and-sword.co.uk

Contents

Acknowledgements

The photographs contained in this volume are largely from the private archive of images I have collected of Luftwaffe aircraft downed in Britain during the period 1939–1945. However, a great many friends and colleagues have assisted me in my quest for such photographs, or otherwise provided additional information. In no particular order of merit, I would like to thank:

Peter Cornwell, Steve Hall, Chris Goss, Dennis Knight, Winston Ramsey, Phillipa Hodgkiss, Alfred Price and Martin Mace.

In addition, I must mention two other fellow researchers who are no longer with us but whose work added considerably to our sum of knowledge relating to the recovery of aircraft wrecks in wartime Britain. They are my late friend Pat Burgess, and a colleague of many years, Peter Foote. Pat had been a prodigious collector of information relating to the county of Sussex, the area in which much of the activity described in this book took place. Peter Foote had been equally industrious in recording the minutiae of events during the Battle of Britain and the Blitz across Britain since the late 1940s and his tireless research work has left a legacy of unequalled information. Had he not recorded some of these events before it was too late to find the evidence then our knowledge of that period would be much the poorer. In many cases, he put considerable historical detail and context to photographs that would otherwise have been a rather less informative record of the momentous events they depicted.

Lastly, I feel I should mention the late Kenneth Watkins. Ken was a collector of Luftwaffe aircraft crash photographs and after his death I was fortunate to be able to acquire his large collection. Ken's photographs complemented and added to those already in my own archive but I was able to extensively draw upon that resource in compiling this book.

In addition, I must extend my thanks to any other individuals and organisations who may have assisted me in over forty years of research and whom I may have inadvertently overlooked. My thanks to you all.

Introduction

The story of the Battle of Britain is well known and recorded in very considerable detail in countless books on the subject. It is not my intention to re-tell that story here. In this volume we will take a pictorial look at the cost to the Luftwaffe bomber force of waging war against the British Isles during the summer of 1940.

What we now know as the Battle of Britain was fought between 10 July and 31 October 1940, although those were artificial dates created post-war by the Air Ministry and were set as being the 'official' period during which the major part of that campaign was fought. However, and in order to set the scene, I have looked briefly at the run-up to the commencement of 'battle proper' but have then examined pictorially each month from July to October 1940. Whilst the cut-off date for the cessation of the battle is officially 31 October 1940, this was not the cessation of German air attacks against Britain. Far from it. It was only the end of the 'official' period of the Battle of Britain. Then the German air assault melded and changed from the mainly daylight campaign, into the day and night blitz, and then to the blitz by night only, followed later in the war by tip-and-run attacks and various periods of other raids employing a variety of tactics, aircraft and weapons. So, whilst this particular volume looks at Luftwaffe bomber actions and their related losses during the Battle of Britain there will be other follow-up titles by the same author in this series and these will cover all other elements and periods of Luftwaffe attacks on Britain, right up until the cessation of hostilities.

The photographs used in this work are drawn from my private archive and provide a fair representation of the losses sustained in terms of aircraft type and geographic location. The majority of action during the Battle of Britain was across the south of England, predominantly in Kent, Sussex, Hampshire, Essex and London, and it is therefore inevitable that the picture content reflects a geographic 'bias' towards the Home County region. However, where photographs are to hand of losses in other parts of the British Isles, a conscious effort has been made to include them.

For the most part, the pictures used in this book were taken by official photographers working for regional and national newspapers or by photo agencies and their contracted photographers. Some were taken by photographers working for the RAF or the Air Ministry. In many cases, the organisations concerned are long defunct, but the images taken by or for such organisations have been collected and preserved across many years by enthusiasts, researchers and historians. Some of the photographs used are from the original official prints, others are from illegally-taken pictures by civilians or military personnel – it being contrary to the Control of Photography Order 1939 for unauthorised persons to take photographs of military subjects. Quite apart from the wartime shortages of film and materials, private photographers faced the danger that if they took their films to chemists or photographic stores, the subject matter might be reported to the Police. Additionally, some photographs used here are from the collections of Luftwaffe participants in the Battle of Britain. In many cases, the photographs will not have been widely seen, if at all, before publication in this volume.

It is true to say that for the first time in modern history the British public were exposed during the Second World War to the frontline realities of war and it was inevitable that photographers would seize upon the opportunity to record the myriad scenes that unfolded. Mostly, photographers were on the spot some while after the initial drama of an enemy aircraft crash, although the scenes they recorded were often powerful and certainly historically important. Without a doubt, the Battle of Britain has become very much a part of the British psyche – fact, fiction, folklore and legend. Here, though, we see the recorded 'fact' of contemporary scenes photo-graphed during that epic summer of 1940. Whilst much that has been written or recorded of the Battle of Britain is subject to debate, discussion, revisionism or even the creation and debunking of myths and misconceptions, there is one simple inescapable fact: the camera never lies. This, then, is a photographic glimpse of the Luftwaffe bomber force during the Battle of Britain, some of the losses the force sustained during the campaign, and some of the faces of the men themselves.

Andy Saunders
East Sussex, October 2013

Chapter One

Prelude to Battle:
October 1939 to June 1940

When the air raid sirens sounded across the British Isles at the declaration of war on Sunday, 3 September 1939 there was an expectation by many that the country would immediately be subjected to mass air attack by German bombers. Although that fear was not realised, it didn't take long for the Luftwaffe to commence air operations against Britain. The Germans didn't yet have bases in France, Belgium, Holland or Norway from which attacks could be mounted, but their bomber aircraft, operating from bases in northern Germany, had the range to reach targets in Scotland and the north of England. For the greater part, though, these regions would be spared the heavy air assault to which the south of the British Isles would be subjected during the summer of 1940.

October 1939 saw the first tentative excursion by the Luftwaffe against the north. These included armed reconnaissance sorties, limited bombing raids, and anti-shipping strikes. On the 16th of that month the first German air attack against Britain was launched by nine Junkers 88 aircraft of I./KG30 against shipping in the Firth of Forth. The next day saw the first enemy aircraft shot down on British soil when another aircraft of I./KG30 was hit by anti-aircraft fire and crashed and exploded on the Isle of Hoy in the Orkneys. Three of the crew were killed and one taken prisoner, wounded. Whilst no photographs of the crash have been traced, the first German aircraft downed on the British mainland was well photographed. This was a Heinkel 111 H-2 of Stab./KG26, shot down at Humbie in the Lammermuir Hills by Spitfires of 602 and 603 Squadrons. Two of the crew were killed, with the other two taken prisoner. Here, crowds flock to view the spectacle of the downed bomber.

THE W\A\R ILLUSTRATED

3d Weekly

Edited by
SIR JOHN HAMMERTON

Editor of 'THE WAR ILLUSTRATED' (1914-1920)
'WORLD WAR, 1914-1918,' 'I WAS THERE!' etc.

First Enemy 'Plane Down in Britain ★ ★ ★ ★ ★ ★ *EXCLUSIVE HISTORIC PHOTOS IN THIS NUMBER*

(*Above*) It was another Heinkel of KG26, this time from the unit's 4th Staffel, that would become the first enemy aircraft downed on English soil since the First World War. This event took place at Bannial Flat Farm, Whitby, on Saturday, 3 February 1940. Here, the aircraft is photographed after coming to rest in the snowy fields close to the farmhouse. Bullet holes pepper the tail and fuselage, testimony to good shooting by Flt Lt P.W. Townsend of 43 Squadron. Together with Fg Off 'Tiger' Folkes and Sgt H.J.L. Hallowes. The three Hurricane pilots had intercepted the Heinkel over the North Sea. In the attack, Uffz R. Leuschake and Uffz J. Meyer were both killed whilst Fw H. Wilms was captured. Another crew member, Uffz K. Missy, was so badly wounded that he later had to have his right leg amputated. Given the raking of the fuselage with gunfire there is surely little wonder at the death and injury that was sustained on board the Heinkel.

(*Opposite page*) Interest in the first German aircraft brought down on the mainland of the British Isles was intense and was covered in detail by all of the main newspapers of the day, as well as the BBC. It also featured on the front cover of the wartime publication *The War Illustrated* which also carried extensive copy on the event under the headline: 'It's Not so Easy to Bomb Britain!'

(*Above*) Six days later and another KG26 Heinkel 111 came to grief over the north of England. This time it was this 5th Staffel machine that was shot down by Sqn Ldr A.D. Farquhar in a 602 Sqn Spitfire whilst en route to attack shipping in the Firth of Forth sea area. The bomber was further attacked by anti-aircraft fire from shipping. In the Spitfire attack, the wireless operator/air gunner, Uffz Franz Weiners, was mortally wounded. The crippled Heinkel ditched its bombs in the sea and at 12.25 hours made a wheels-down landing in a field at Heugh Farm, North Berwick Law, East Lothian, but ran into a hedge and tipped onto its nose. The three other crew members were taken POW.

(*Opposite above*) Despite some damage sustained in the crash landing and fighter attack, the aircraft was repairable and quickly earmarked for evaluation and test flying by the RAF. Carefully dismantled, the Heinkel was made airworthy at RAF Turnhouse and then flown to the Royal Aircraft Establishment, Farnborough. Here, it was painted in British camouflage and given the RAF serial number AW177. Operated by No.1426 Enemy Aircraft Flight at RAF Duxford, the aircraft was eventually lost in a tragic accident at Polebrook when it came into land just as an RAF operated Junkers 88 was using the runway from the opposite direction. The pilot of the Heinkel 111, Fg Off F.A. Barr, opened up the engines and made a steep turn to port but stalled and crashed, whereupon the fuel tanks exploded. Six of the ten on board, including Barr, were killed. Here, looking almost pristine and factory fresh, we see the Heinkel 'under new management'.

(*Opposite below*) The emblem of Kampfgeschwader 26 (KG26) was this seated lion, seen here on the North Berwick Law Heinkel 111. The Latin inscription boldly declares *Vestigium Leonis* – In the Lion's Footprints.

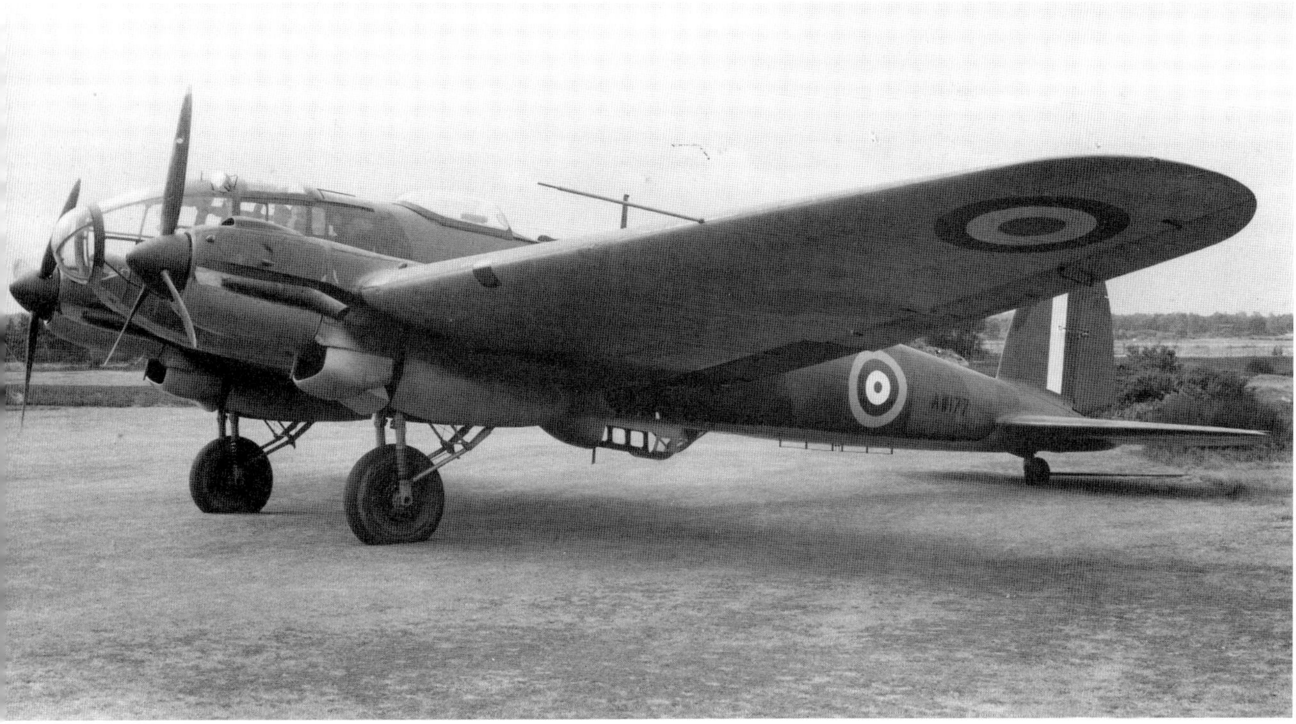

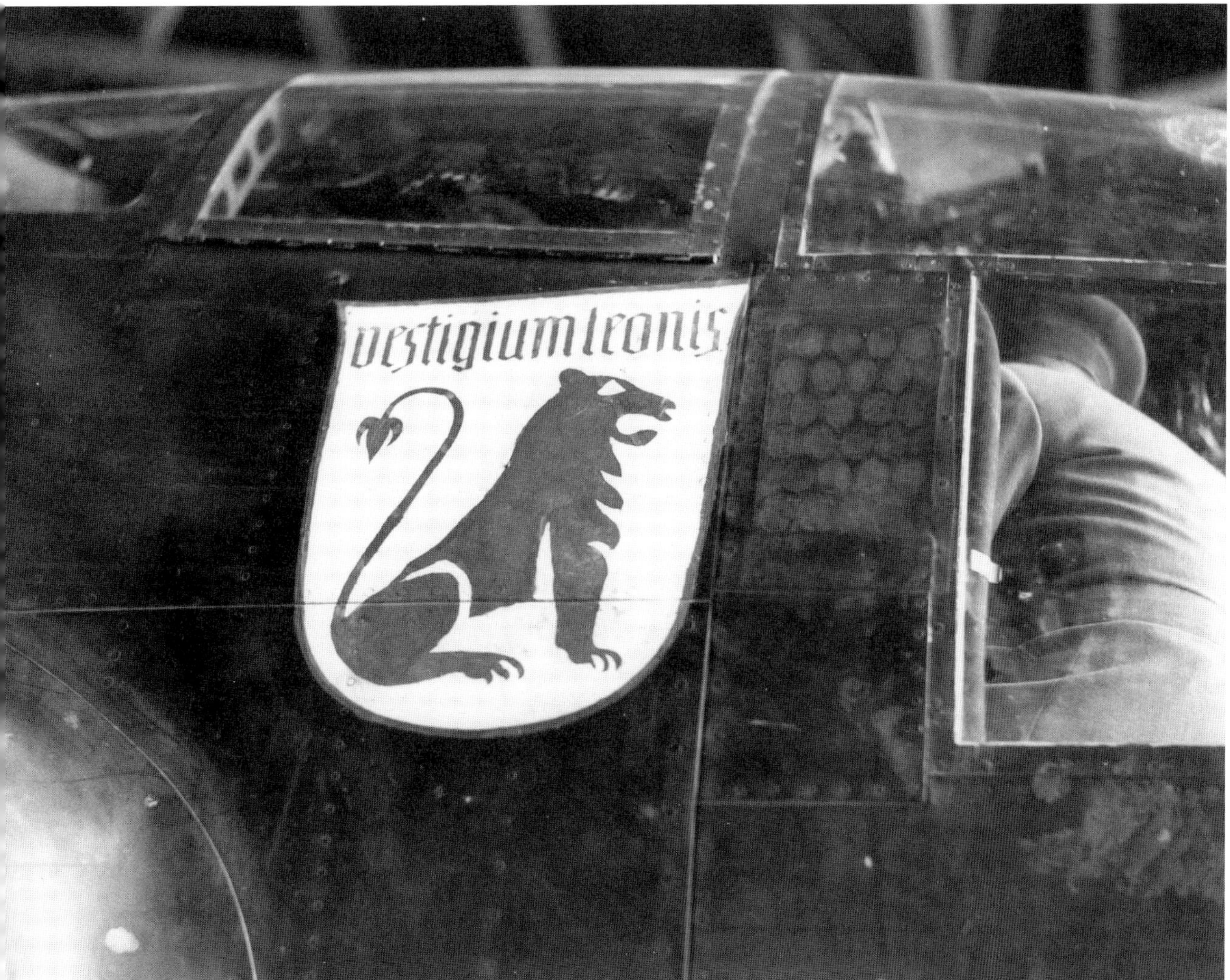
vestigium leonis

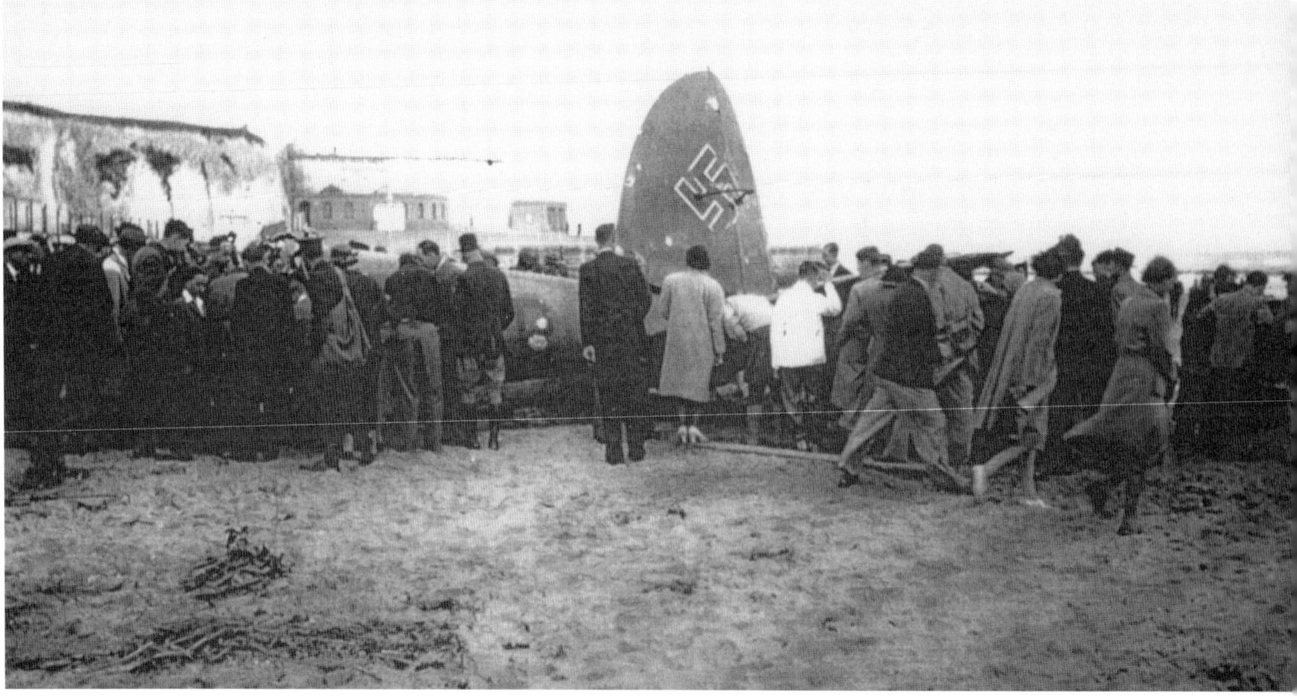

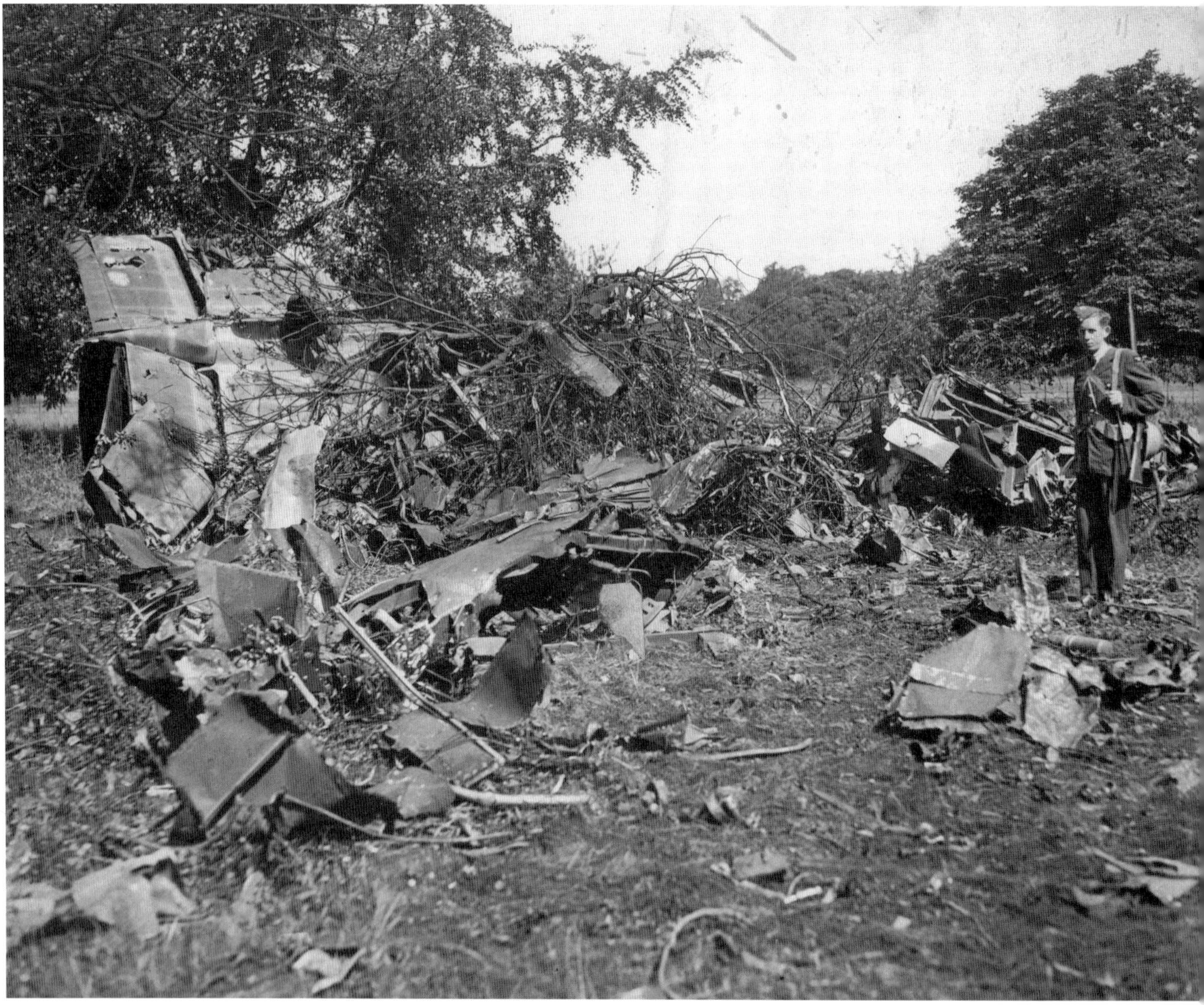

(*Above*) On 3 July 1940 this Dornier 17-Z of 8./KG77 was shot down into a hop garden near Paddock Wood, Kent, by three Hurricanes of 32 Squadron from RAF Biggin Hill. The fuselage has been riddled with bullet holes in a fusillade which killed one of the crew members. Another was killed when the aircraft ploughed into the hop poles. On board were nine 50kg bombs, another six having been dropped by the raider over RAF Kenley, an aerodrome that would come under rather more intensive assault by Dornier 17 aircraft in little over a month.

(*Opposite above*) By June 1940 the Germans were very firmly establishing their presence in France and the Low Countries, thereby giving the Luftwaffe what were in effect forward operating bases from where air operations against Britain could more easily be conducted, and bringing all parts of the islands within easy range. On the night of 18/19 June Heinkel 111 aircraft from elements of KG4 were deployed against targets in mainland Britain. This aircraft of the 6th Staffel, KG4 was lost to a Spitfire of 19 Squadron that was being flown on a night sortie by Fg Off G.E. Ball. Damaged over Colchester, it eventually crashed onto the foreshore below cliffs at Sacketts Gap, Margate, becoming the first of many hundreds of enemy aircraft downed over the county. In this view the wrecked bomber has attracted a considerable crowd, all anxious for their first close-up look at an enemy raider.

(*Opposite below*) That same night, another Heinkel 111 of Stab./KG4 (the staff flight of Kampfgeschwader 4) was shot down and fell into the garden of the Bishop of Chelmsford. The only survivor of this incident was the pilot, Lt Erich Simon, who baled out near Writtle, to be taken POW. The remaining three members of the crew all perished in the aircraft, the wreckage of which was badly broken up and scattered. Here it is being guarded by an RAF airman.

Although not a Luftwaffe bomber, the photograph of this Heinkel 59-B seaplane is certainly relevant within the context of this book. The aircraft type was operated by the Luftwaffe in an air-sea rescue role along the Channel coast and over the North Sea with the Seenotflugkommando 1, based at Boulogne, being responsible for rescuing many ditched German aircrew who otherwise might have perished. These aircraft also rescued many downed RAF aircrew and although these men were taken prisoner they were at least alive. This particular aircraft, painted white and bearing the International Red Cross emblem with German civilian markings, was intercepted by Spitfires of 54 Squadron over the English Channel on 9 July 1940 and forced to land at the Goodwin Sands. Later, it was towed ashore by RNLI Lifeboat and beached at Deal. The view of the Air Ministry was that these aircraft could not be granted immunity from attack since they were Luftwaffe operated, carried defensive armaments and were equipped with radios that might report the position of shipping or other militarily important information. The three crew were captured unharmed on what was the eve of the day later declared to be the very opening of the Battle of Britain: 10 July 1940.

Chapter Two

The Early Skirmishing:
July 1940

On 11 July 1940 this Heinkel 111 of 2./KG55 was shot down by Hurricanes of 145 Squadron from RAF Westhampnett during an attack on Portsmouth. Two of the crew were killed in the fighter attack; the remaining three were wounded but taken POW after the blazing bomber landed on East Beach, Selsey. The captain, Oblt Siegfried Schweinhagen, later wrote: 'Just there, in front of the beach huts, stood five young ladies in bathing costumes, our reception committee, and two elderly men with shotguns who came to ward off the threatened invasion of the evil Hun! Then, a last handshake and the crew who had been together on over eighty operations over Poland, France and England, had to part. Our brave Heinkel could not bear to see us part, and with a huge explosion the fire that had smouldered in an engine found its way to the fuel tanks. For us, the war was over.' In this photograph, signed by Siegfried Schweinhagen, the fire takes hold as brass-helmeted firemen stand and watch, along with inquisitive locals.

RAF airmen and soldiers pick amongst the charred cinders of the Heinkel at East Beach, Selsey. Until very recently, molten globules of alloy that had solidified amongst the pebbles could still be found at the crash site.

Two days later another Heinkel 111 of KG55, this time from the unit's Staff Flight (Stab.), was intercepted by Hurricanes of 43 Squadron from RAF Tangmere during an armed reconnaissance sortie to Southampton. Dumping its bomb load, the crippled aircraft made a good forced landing in a Hampshire meadow beside the Hambleton to Farnham road at Hipley, just opposite the Horse and Jockey pub. One of the crew had been killed, three others injured and one escaped unharmed.

Rushing from his pub the landlord of the Horse and Jockey, Mr Percy H. Tibble, captured the surviving crew armed with his son's old toy pistol! Here, for the benefit of the photographer, he tells his bar staff and son how he did it.

At the other end of the British Isles, and on the same day, another of KG26's Heinkel 111 aircraft came off worst from an encounter with the three Spitfires of Yellow Section, 603 Squadron, who shot down this 9th Staffel aircraft over Aberdeen, sending it crashing into the city's South Anderson Drive Ice Rink after it had bombed the Hall Russell shipyards. All four crew were killed in the crash.

An RAF Queen Mary low-loader takes the scorched and battered wing sections of the Heinkel 111 away from the ice rink.

On 20 July 1940 this Junkers 88 of 4(F)./122 took off from Brussels for a reconnaissance sortie over the east coast of England but was intercepted by three Hurricanes of 56 Squadron from RAF North Weald which shot the intruder down at Cockett Wick Farm, St Osyth, Essex. The aircraft burnt out, and the crew of four were captured.

(*Right*) One of the crew members taken POW at St Osyth that day was the radio operator, Ogefr Walter Plock.

(*Below*) Yet another Luftwaffe reconnaissance sortie that ended up on a one-way journey to England for both aircraft and crew was this Dornier 17-M that was out observing road and rail traffic along the south coast of England. Shot down by Hurricanes of 238 Squadron the aircraft crashed in flames and burned out at Nutford Farm, Blandford, Dorset, on 21 July 1940. The three crew were captured, all of them wounded. An oily black pall of smoke coils upwards into the summer sky, captured by a fortuitously passing photographer.

(*Above*) One of the crew, Uffz Albert Werner, was seriously injured and is seen here on a stretcher at the scene as first aid is administered.

(*Opposite above*) The destruction of enemy aircraft was not always without cost to defending fighters, and in this instance a Hurricane collided with the bomber causing the death of the RAF pilot. The Junkers 88, of 5./KG51, had been tasked to attack the Gloster Aircraft Factory at Hucclecote, Gloucestershire, on 25 July 1940 when it was intercepted by two Hurricanes of the Airfield Defence Flight, No.4 Ferry Pilot's Pool, RAF Kemble. Pilot Officers R.G. Manlove and C.A. Bird intercepted the Junkers, but in the attack Plt Off Bird collided with the bomber's tail causing the enemy to crash at Lower Weir Farm, Oakridge, Gloucestershire. The four-man crew of the Junkers 88 baled out, although one of them was killed when his parachute failed to open. It was Plt Off Bird who was killed in the collision.

(*Opposite below*) Elsewhere that day, this Dornier 17-M of Stab./StG1 was on a reconnaissance mission for the Stuka Geschwader to which it was attached but ran into three Spitfires of 152 Squadron, meeting its fiery end as a consequence of that encounter at East Fleet Farm, Fleet, Dorset. One of the crew was killed, but the remaining two were captured, one of them wounded. Flying reconnaissance sorties like this against the British Isles was clearly a hazardous undertaking for the Luftwaffe crews assigned that task.

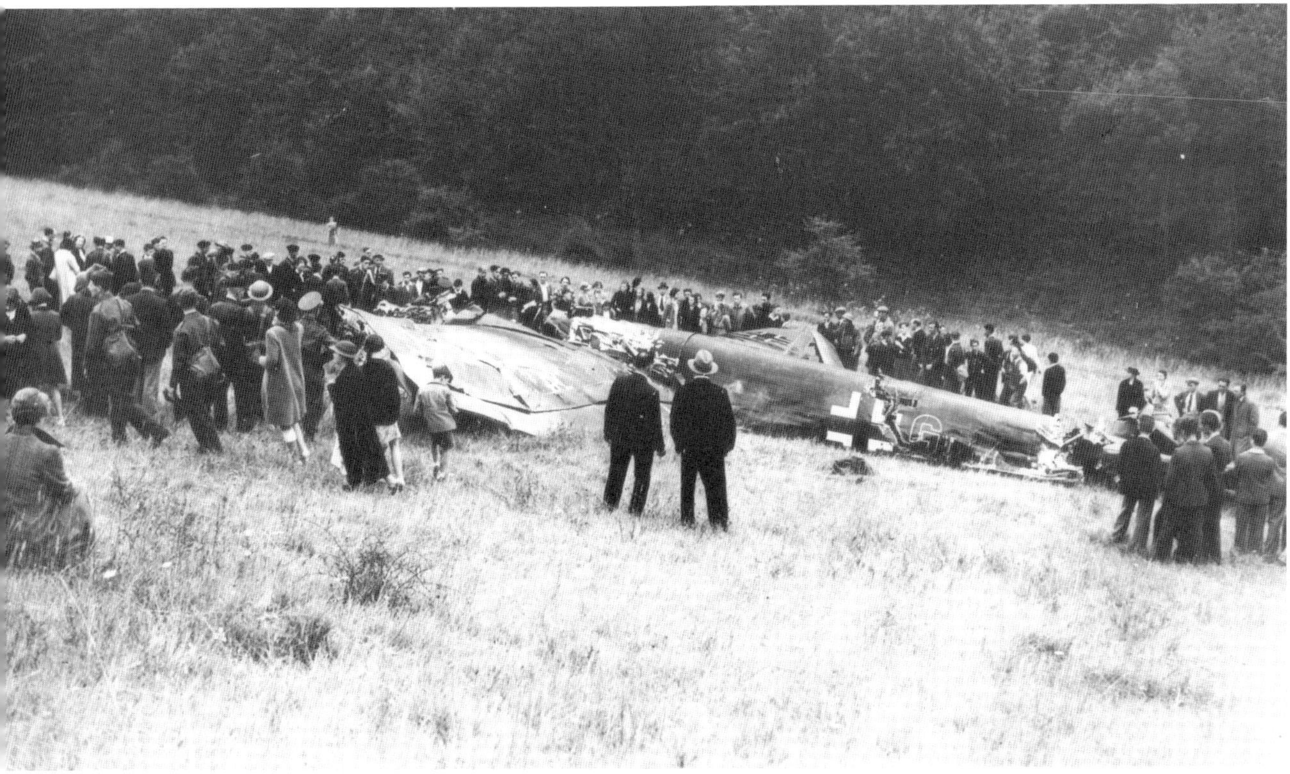

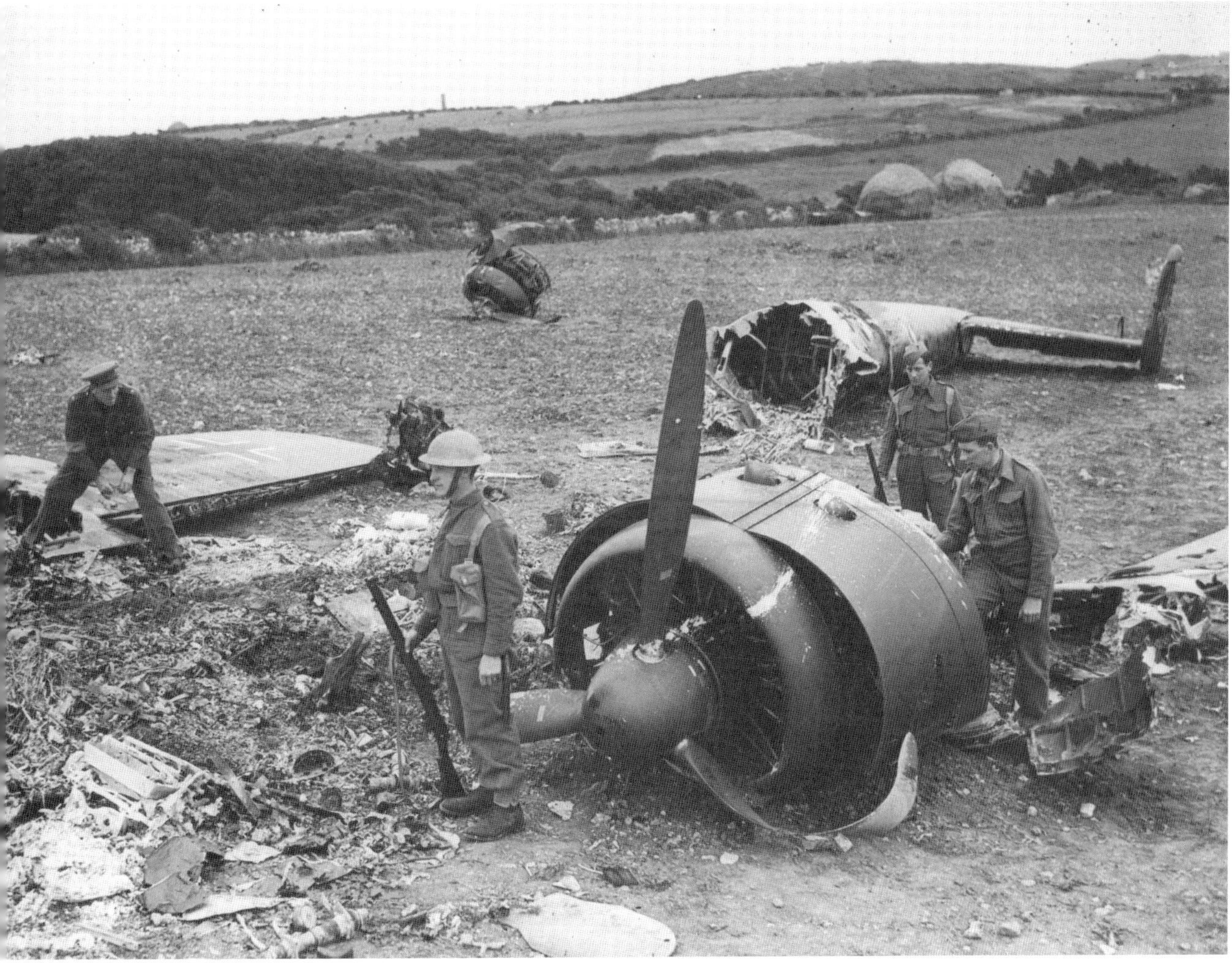

(*Above*) Sometimes, the hazards of operational flying over enemy territory were rather less obvious. This Heinkel 111 of 1./KG4 was lost due to an unexplained on-board explosion on 26 July 1940 whilst on a mine laying sortie between Lyme Regis and Sidmouth. Only one survivor out of the crew of five emerged from this rather crumpled wreckage, with a wounded Uffz Georg Strickstrock being taken into custody by farmer Mr B.J. Parsons after the aircraft impacted into one of his fields at Longfield Farm, Smeathorpe, Devon.

(*Opposite above*) The cause of the demise of this Junkers 88 of 3./KG51 was also rather less obvious to RAF intelligence officers investigating its arrival in Britain. In fact, the aircraft was on a bombing sortie to Crewe on 28 July 1940 when it became lost due to a failure in its direction-finding equipment. As a consequence, it wandered as far as Dublin before taking an easterly track which took it back directly over London which they mistook for Paris. Heading south, the crew were somewhat puzzled to discover the English Channel and, short on fuel, had no option but to land, which they did at Buckholt Farm, Sidley, in East Sussex. All four crew members were captured unharmed and the men from the locally based 302 Searchlight Battery, Royal Artillery, later posed with the downed bomber. One of them, having fired at the Junkers 88 with his Lewis gun as it came in for its forced landing, claimed to have shot it down! Carefully dismantled, the aircraft was later repaired and test flown by the RAF like the Heinkel 111 downed at North Berwick Law in February.

(*Opposite below*) Almost inevitably, Luftwaffe aircrew shot down over Britain were immediately captured and taken POW, or else they quickly gave themselves up. An exception to that general rule involved the crew of a Heinkel 111 of 8./KG55 brought down by anti-aircraft fire over Bristol on 29 July and abandoned by its five crew members over Newbury, Berkshire. The aircraft itself fell at Fullers Lane, Newbury, where it exploded and totally disintegrated. Investigators found no bodies in the wreckage and this begged a question that wasn't immediately answered; where were the crew?

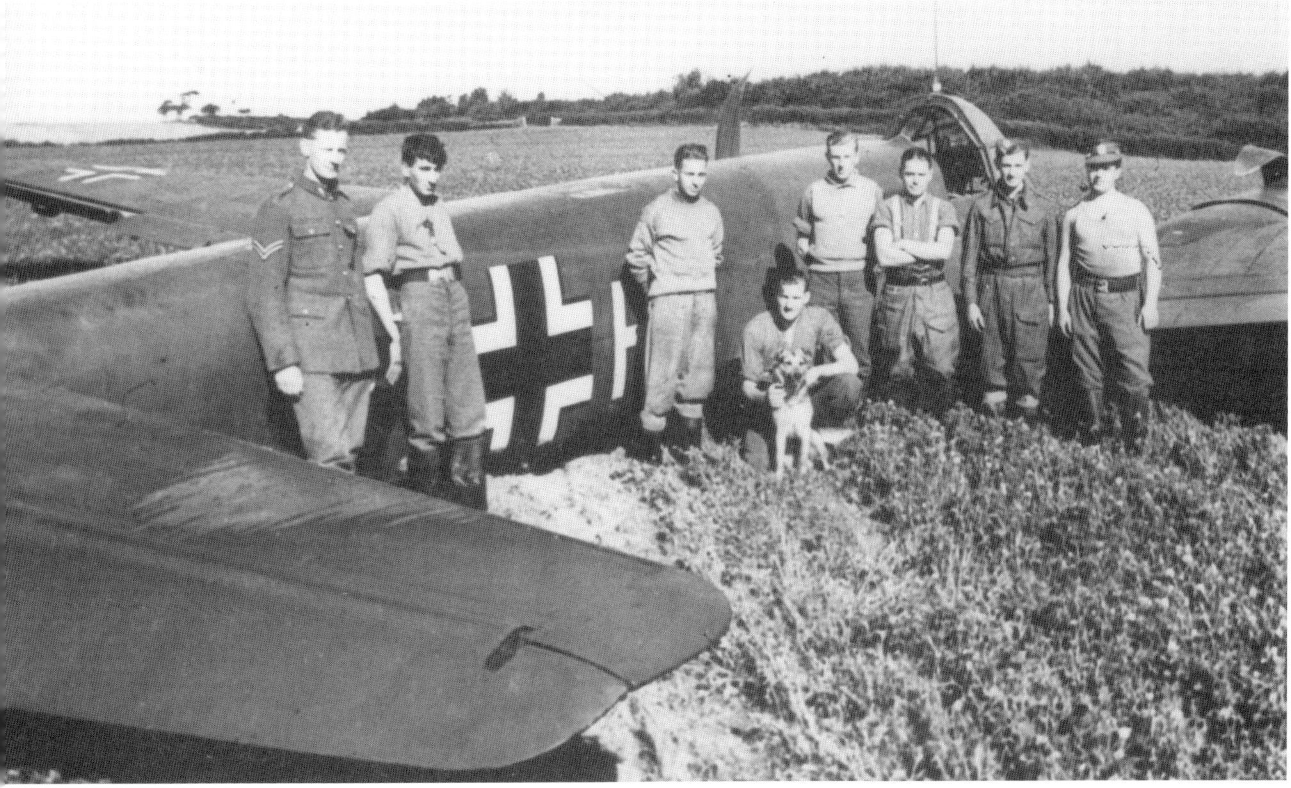

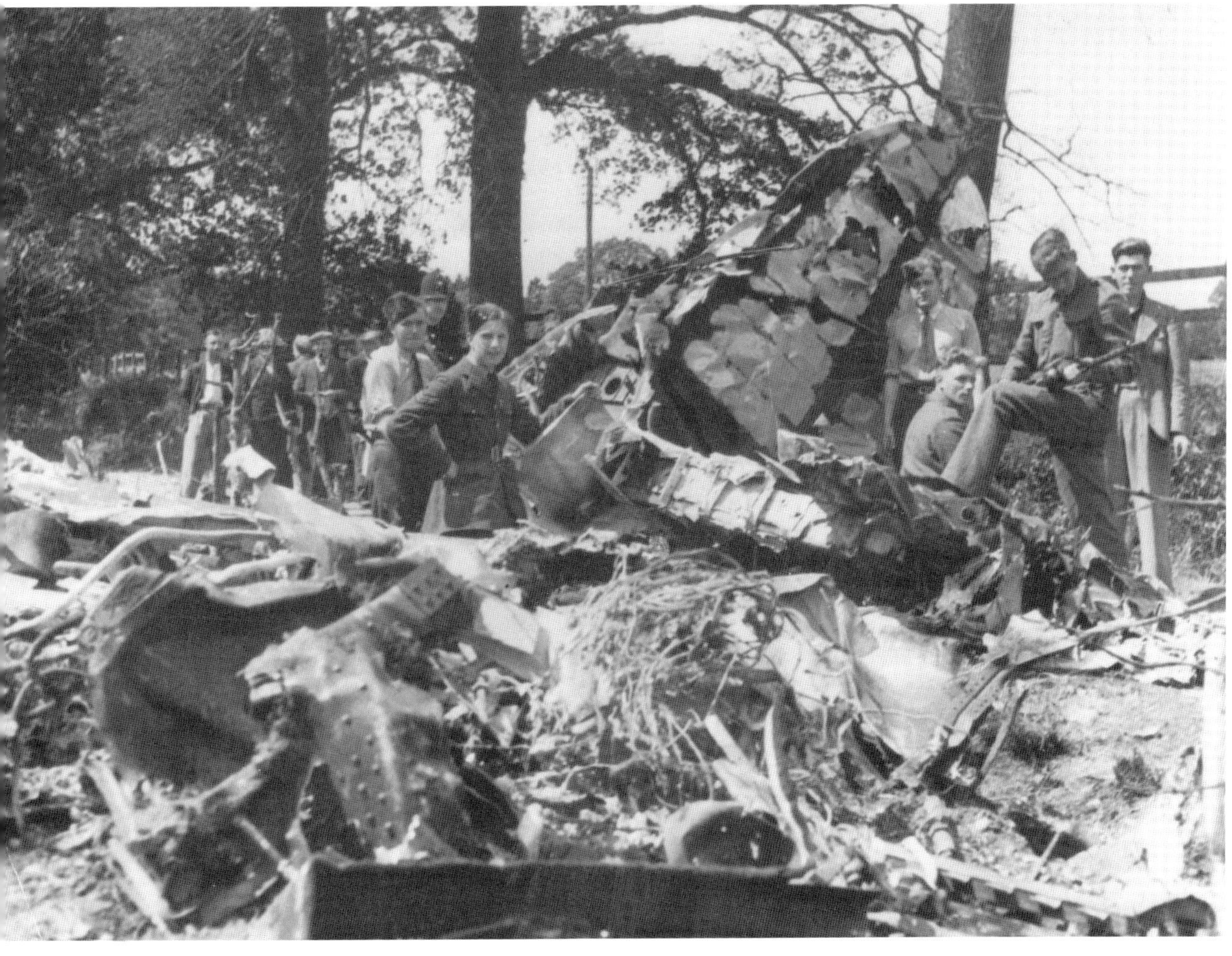

Having drifted down on their parachutes, the five Germans expected almost immediate capture. Remarkably, only Uffz Kurt Boker and Fw Theodor Metzner were captured fairly quickly. Of the others, Gefr Heinz Morgenthal and Gefr Ernst Ostheimer were captured after forty-eight hours at large, but Fw Josef Markl evaded capture for a remarkable nine days. This was a record time for a downed Luftwaffe airman to be at large in Britain, his evasion resulting in a huge manhunt by Police and the military. He was eventually spotted by a Lady Buckland who ordered her chauffeur, Mr E. Nicholls, to stop and drive the airman to Newbury Police Station. Exhausted and hungry, Josef Markl apparently offered no resistance to the suggestion that he should take a ride with Lady Buckland. It must have been the most unusual capture of an enemy airman in Britain. Here, Gefr Ernst Ostheimer poses for the camera during a day-trip to the Channel Islands shortly before he was shot down.

Seeing out July 1940, a Junkers 88 of 7./KG4 was observed flying low and on fire over Bury St Edmunds, Suffolk, during the early hours of 30 July 1940. Moments later it struck an oak tree and exploded violently, killing all four crew members instantly. Wreckage was strewn across several acres and this charred tail section was about the only recognisable piece of Junkers 88 that remained. As the Battle of Britain moved on into its second month, so the pace would now increase from the rather sporadic engagements and sorties that had typified Luftwaffe operations over Britain during July.

Chapter Three

The Heat of Summer and the Heat of Battle: August 1940

August opened quietly, with the first enemy aircraft that was downed 'on British territory' being a Heinkel 115-C seaplane, one of a pair of such aircraft which attacked Convoy FN239 south of Aberdeen shortly after midnight on 2 August 1940. Bizarrely, one of the aircraft struck the lifeboat davit on the SS *Highlander* and crashed onto the deck of the vessel killing the crew of three. The second aircraft was shot down into the sea by anti-aircraft fire, again with the loss of its crew. Later, the ship sailed into Leith harbour with its 'prize' on the deck.

Gradually, the tempo of air attacks against Britain increased. At first, the Luftwaffe concentrated on coastal convoys, shipping and port installations and this Junkers 88 of Stab./II.KG54 was engaged in an attack against Portland naval base when it was intercepted and shot down by a Hurricane of 213 Squadron, crashing at Blacknore Fort, Portland Head, on 11 August 1940. The four crew were captured. The captain of the aircraft, Oblt Karl Wette was badly wounded and he features in the photograph on page 88. Here, the aircraft attracts interest from soldiers and locals, as white-overalled technicians begin the process of examination and dismantling.

This Junkers 88 of 3./KG51, carrying the markings 9K+EL (No. 3134), is photographed here at its home base on Melun airfield to the south of Paris. The picture was taken shortly before the aircraft took off for an attack on Portsmouth Harbour on 12 August 1940.

(*Above*) The next photographs of 9K + EL, 3134, were taken when it was no more than a heap of wreckage in a field at Horsepasture Farm, Rowlands Castle, shortly after noon on 12 August. According to RAF intelligence reports the aircraft exploded in mid-air, with the rear canopy and gun falling to earth outside the operations room at nearby RAF Thorney Island. Three of the crew were killed, but the fourth landed, wounded, at Hayling Island. Here, two nurses pose with the crumpled tail unit of the bomber.

(*Opposite above*) The main body of the aircraft fell nearby, inverted, and was guarded by RAF airmen. As with the Junkers 88 down at Sidley on 28 July, a Bombardier of the Royal Artillery, Ernest Bridgeman, claimed to have downed the aircraft with machine gun fire, although this can be discounted. Bridgeman later found himself before the Chichester County Magistrates charged with illegally photographing the wreck after having been stopped by PC Sidney Reynolds and the camera confiscated. When the magistrates heard the story about Bridgeman shooting the bomber down, they dismissed the case, complimented the Royal Artilleryman on his shooting and photography and returned the pictures to him. As we will see on 8 October 1940, PC Reynolds himself struggled over strict adherence to the rules and regulations concerning downed German aircraft (page 106).

(*Opposite below*) 'Eagle Day' (Adler Tag) was the day the Luftwaffe launched what was intended to be its knock-out air operation against the RAF: 13 August 1940. It was a day of somewhat limited success for the Germans, and also a day when their bomber force suffered grievously. One of the casualties was this Dornier 17-Z of Stab./KG2, shot down over the Thames estuary by a Spitfire as it approached its target at RAF Eastchurch. Three of the crew were wounded, but all four men escaped alive. Quite how any of them survived this crumpled wreck on the railway bank at Pherbec Bridge, Barham, Kent, is hard to fathom.

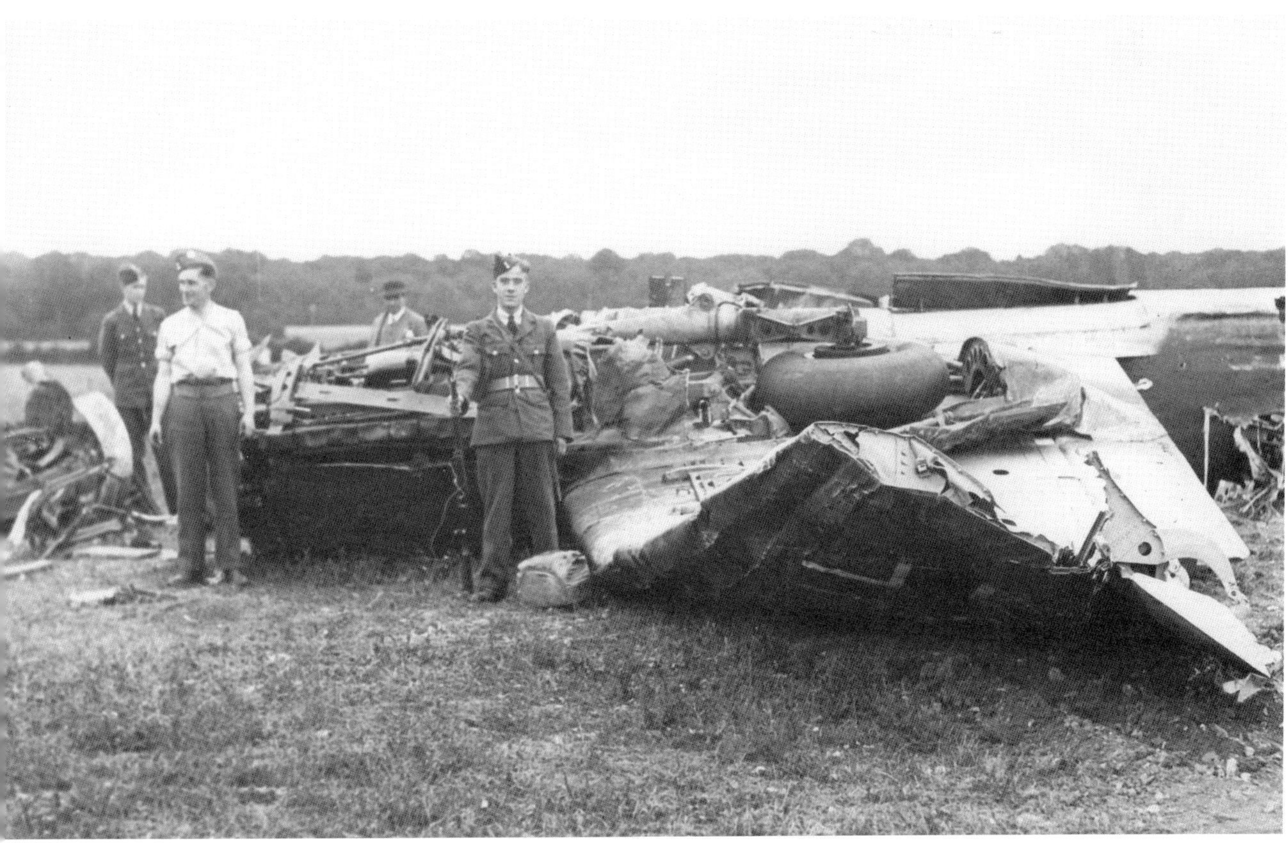

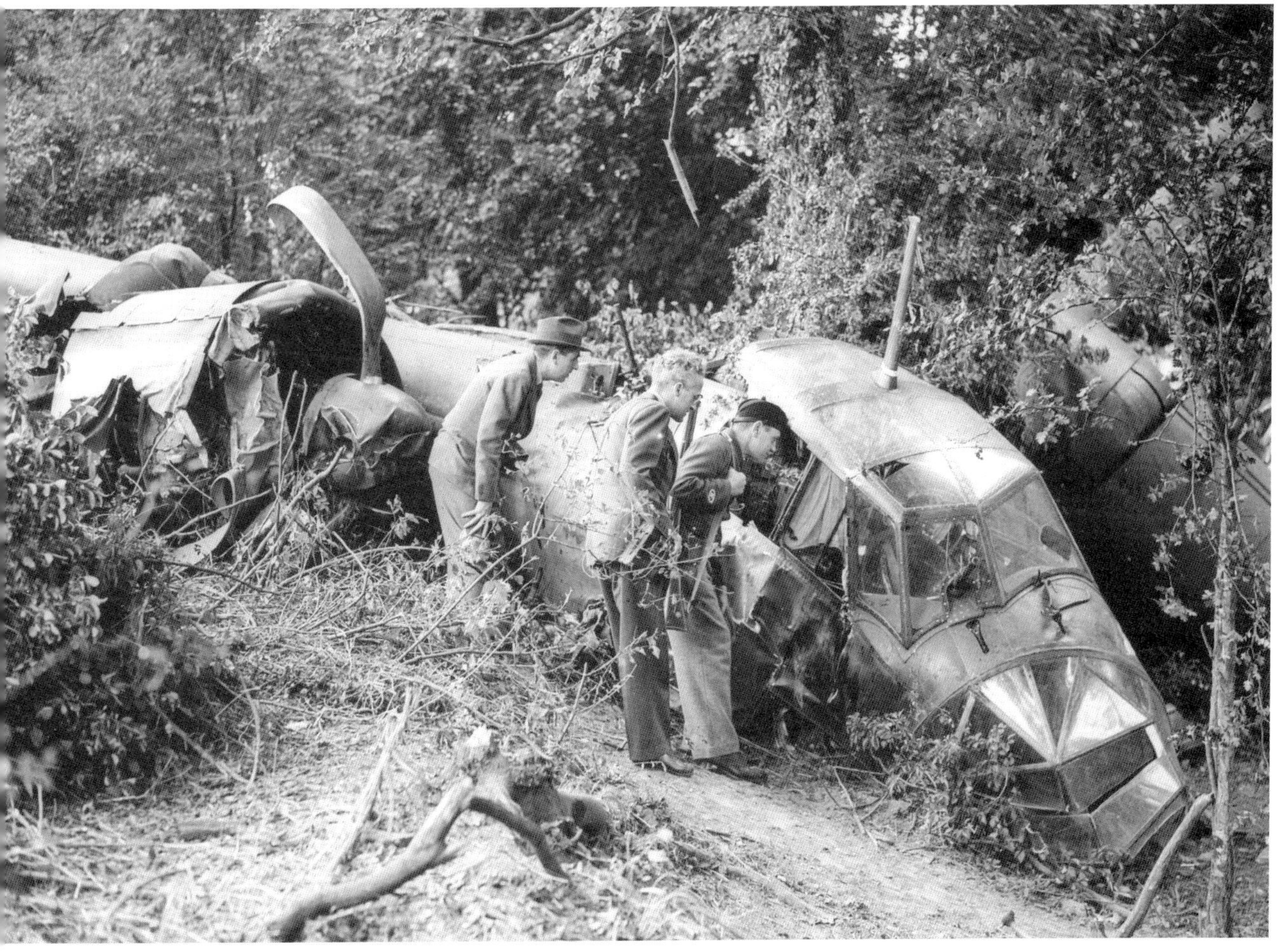

Another of the KG2 raiders that didn't get home that day was this one that smashed itself to pieces when shot down onto mudflats at Seasalter, Kent. The four crew members, from 8./KG2, baled out very low, with three of them being killed and the fourth captured badly hurt. The soldier to the left seems to be examining a map or document he has found in the wreckage. The posts in the distance are anti-invasion glider landing obstacles.

Rather more intact than the two KG2 Dornier 17s in the previous images, this one from 7./KG2 ended up making a respectable belly landing in a field at Stodmarsh, Kent, on 13 August 1940 after having one engine put out of action in an attack by RAF fighters and taking hits in petrol and oil feeds. The four crew members were captured, one of them wounded. Noteworthy are the scribbled lines on this photograph, fore and aft of the fuselage cross. This was inscribed on the original press photograph by the official censor who wished to remove identification markings that may have been helpful to the Germans in determining what had happened to one of their aircraft.

Further west, 'Adler Tag' raiders were also having a bad time with the Junkers 88s of KG54, taking a mauling as they crossed the coast near Littlehampton. One, an aircraft of Stab.II./KG54, was shot down by Hurricanes of 43 Squadron, falling into Swanbourne Lake at Arundel Castle. Of the crew, two baled out and were captured unhurt whilst another was dragged to his death when his parachute caught on the tail of the Junkers 88. The fourth landed in a tree, mortally wounded, and died in hospital two days later. The aircraft smashed itself to pieces in woodland on the slopes above the lake, with much of the wreckage cascading down into the water. Here, soldiers examine the remains of an engine and an undercarriage leg that have lodged on the pathway running alongside the western edge of the lake. Maps and documents were recovered from the wreckage and taken to nearby RAF Tangmere to await collection by an RAF Intelligence Officer, but before they could be inspected they were destroyed in a dive bombing attack on the airfield.

(*Above*) The aircraft was heading for its target at Farnborough when it was intercepted and crashed with its full bomb load. Unknown to the soldiers standing on the path in the photograph on page 31, an unexploded 250kg bomb lies buried in the disturbed chalk immediately in front of where they stand. The bomb lay undiscovered until 1990, its rusting nose protruding unseen from the chalk bank amongst tree roots. For sixty years, sightseers and walkers had strolled inches away from the nose of the bomb at this well visited beauty spot. Investigators then found three other unexploded 50kg bombs nearby, and all were dealt with by bomb disposal teams. This photograph shows the 250kg bomb having its explosive content steamed out and neutralised.

(*Opposite above*) A few miles further inland, a Junkers 88 of Stab.I./KG54 was also caught by 43 Squadron's Hurricanes and in a brief engagement the bomber's pilot, Oblt Josef Oestermann, was shot dead with a bullet wound to his head. With the aircraft out of control, the other three crew members rapidly baled out of the uncontrolled bomber and were captured unhurt. Meanwhile, the Junkers 88 crashed violently to earth at Phillis Wood, Treyford, and exploded on impact. Fire then consumed what little was left. Of Josef Oestermann, no trace was ever found.

(*Opposite below, left*) Oblt Josef Oestermann.

(*Opposite below, right*) The crash site is literally on the path of the South Downs Way national trail, where walkers pass a memorial to this still officially 'missing' Luftwaffe pilot.

IN MEMORIAM
HAUPTMANN
JOSEPH OESTERMANN
PILOT KG54 STAB
1919 ✝ 1940

Leutnant zur See (naval Lieutenant) Wilhelm Brinkbaumer was another Junkers 88 crewman lost on 13 August when his aircraft was shot down by a Hurricane of 257 Squadron at Sidlesham, West Sussex, the aircraft exploding on impact. Brinkbaumer, a naval officer attached to a Luftwaffe unit, was serving with 8./LG1 and was killed along with the three other crew members during a sortie to bomb Andover. Although no photographs of the crashed aircraft have yet been identified, this was Lt zur See Brinkbaumer. He was buried at St Andrew's Church, Tangmere, where his body still rests. Above shows the memorial card with its photograph of the original grave marker that was sent to the Brinkbaumer family via the Red Cross.

(*Opposite page*) Karl-Wilhelm Brinkbaumer's grave today in Tangmere Churchyard.

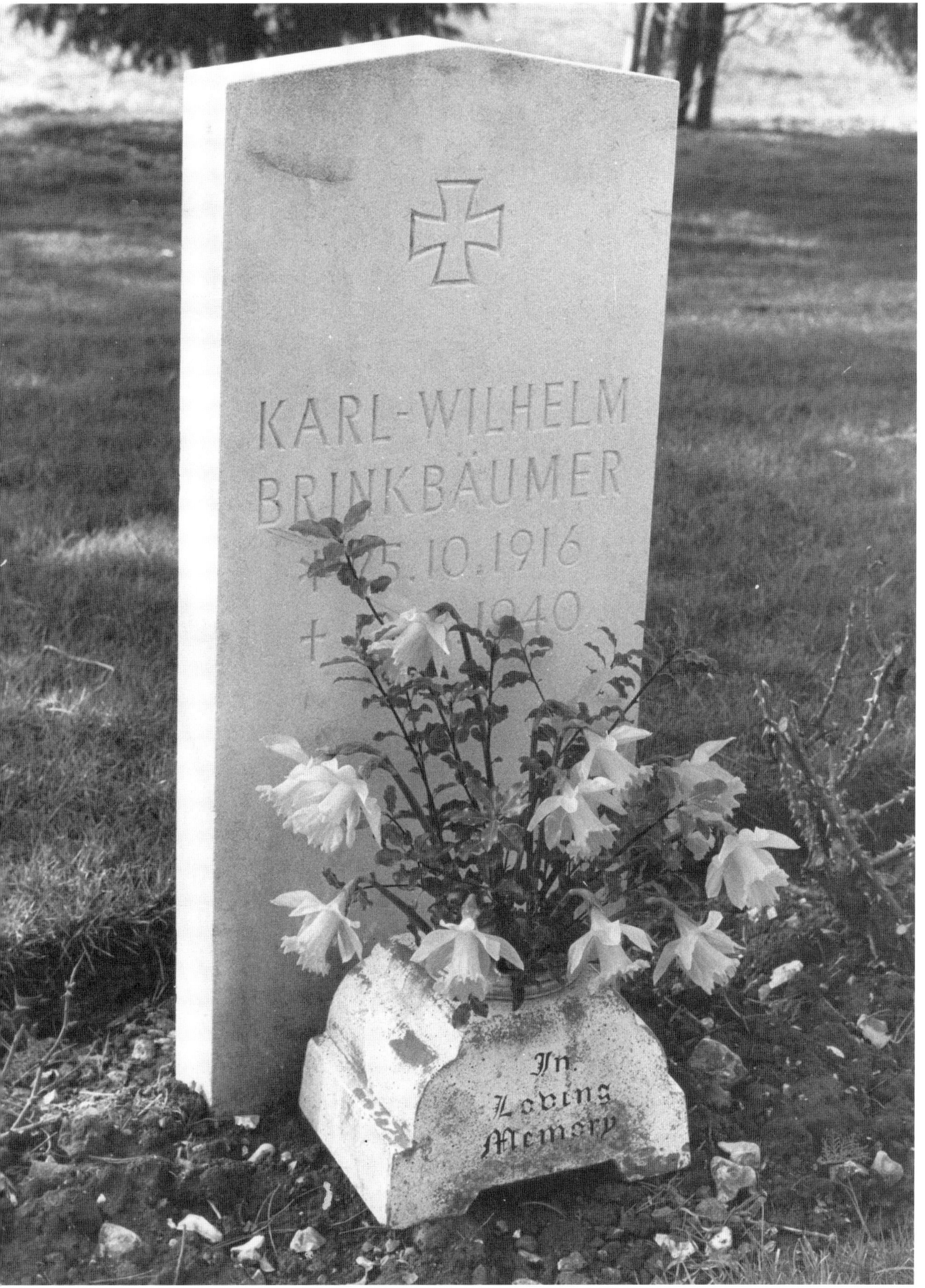
KARL-WILHELM
BRINKBÄUMER
In Loving Memory

(*Left*) Another of the casualties in the 8./LG1 Junkers 88 brought down at Sidlesham was Major Alfons Scheuplein who also lies buried at Tangmere. Here, he is photographed returning from an earlier raid.

(*Right*) This is Gefr Otto Röger, another member of the same Junkers 88 crew. He lies at St Andrew's Churchyard, Tangmere, together with Brinkbaumer, Scheuplein and the fourth crew member, Gefr Josef Dietl, of whom no photograph has yet been traced.

(*Above*) There was some degree of respite in Luftwaffe air operations on 14 August 1940 after the maximum effort of the previous twenty-four hours, although some sporadic activity during the day over the western part of the country saw the Heinkel 111s of KG27 in action. One of these, a machine from 8./KG27, was engaged on operations over the west of England when it was intercepted, first by Hurricanes of 213 Squadron and then by three Spitfire pilots of a non-frontline unit, No. 7 Operational Training Unit. Like the two pilots who downed the Junkers 88 at Oakridge on 25 July, Wing Commander J. Hallings-Pott, Sqn Ldr J. McLean and Plt Off P. Ayerst did not 'qualify' as Battle of Britain pilots under subsequent Air Ministry rules, and yet all three participated in an action during the period of the battle that resulted in the destruction of an enemy aircraft. The five crew members of the Heinkel set fire to their aircraft after making a forced landing at Border House Farm near Chester at around 9.00pm. Only the bullet-holed rear fuselage and outer wing sections survived, relatively intact.

(*Opposite below*) Apart from the human cost to the Luftwaffe, the cost of German air raids against Britain are powerfully portrayed in this photograph of a mass burial service at Maidstone, Kent, for the victims of Junkers 87 'Stuka' dive-bombing attack against RAF Detling, a Coastal Command aerodrome. In total, twenty-four service personnel were killed along with three civilians. A great many more were injured. The station was devastated in the raid, and amongst the deaths was that of the CO of RAF Detling, Gp Capt E.P. Meggs Davies. Forty dive-bombers delivered over 200 bombs in a raid lasting several minutes which destroyed or damaged most of the buildings on the airfield and also wrecked twenty Avro Anson aircraft. The raiding force was not intercepted, and carried out the attack unhindered and without loss.

(*Above*) 11-year-old schoolgirls Wendy Anderton and Cathie Jones point out some of the bullet holes in the Heinkel. Their respective fathers, farmer Mr Anderton and butcher Mr Jones, both of them Home Guardsmen, captured the crew who were then taken into the farmhouse where tea was prepared for them by Wendy and Cathie. With a name like Mr Jones, and being both a butcher and Home Guardsmen, it is almost tempting to wonder if he might have said: 'Don't panic, Mr Anderton, don't panic!'

(*Opposite page*) Another KG27 Heinkel that made a one-way journey to Britain that day was one of three 9./KG27 aircraft that were sortied to attack Cardiff Docks during the early evening of 14 August 1940. Intercepted over the Cotswolds by Spitfires of 92 Squadron before reaching its objective, this aircraft was shot down by Flt Lt R.R.S. Tuck who disabled both engines. Slithering across a meadow at Charterhouse Farm, near Cheddar in Somerset, the landing run ended in a collision with a dry stone wall bordering a country lane. The five crew stepped out, shaken but unharmed, and into at least five years of captivity. This is the Charterhouse Farm Heinkel, its Perspex nose glazing broken by the combined battering of bullets and bits of stone wall. Souvenir hunters have doubtless also played their part, as Perspex was a much sought after commodity from crashed aircraft for the purpose of making rings, brooches, models and other keepsakes.

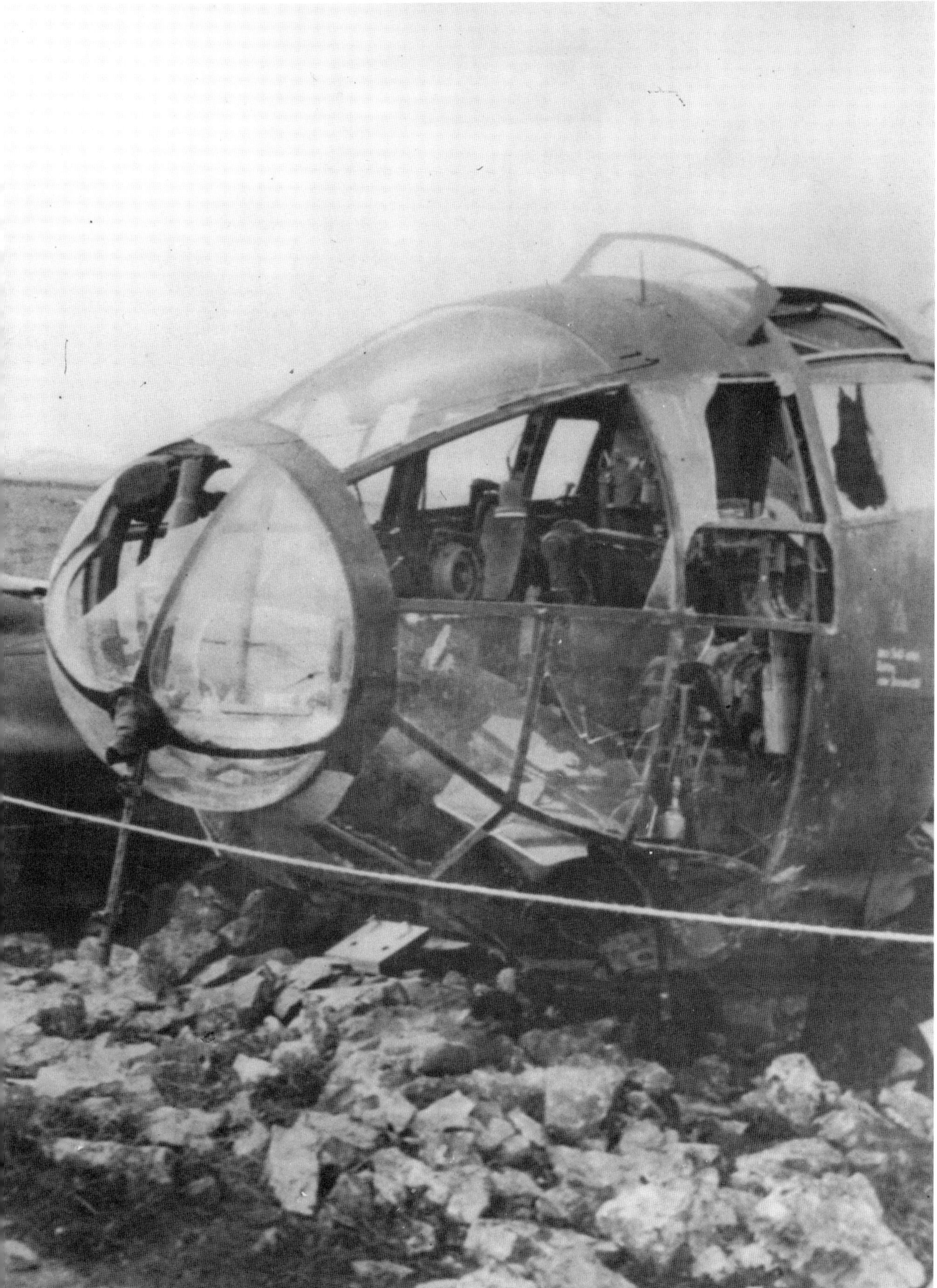

The second of the three aircraft from 9./KG27 was shot down at Canns Farm, Puriton, Somerset, by Spitfire pilots Flt Lt R.R.S. Tuck and Plt Off W.C. Watling of 92 Squadron with all the crew baling out and taken into captivity, one of them wounded. The aircraft smashed itself to pieces, probably leaving a good few bits of shattered Perspex for souvenir hunters to collect. The third aircraft in this raiding force was also shot down by 92 Squadron, crashing into the sea at Bridgewater Bay with the loss of all five crew members.

Generally, most people would associate the Messerschmitt 110 with being principally a heavy fighter in the Luftwaffe's equipment inventory during 1940. In fact, in its Messerschmitt 110-D version it was employed as a bomber aircraft and was used specifically in this role during the Battle of Britain by one particular unit, Erprobungsgruppe 210. On 14 August 1940 the unit took part in a dive-bombing attack on RAF Manston, Kent, during which one of the attacking aircraft took a direct hit from a Bofors 40mm anti-aircraft shell. The pilot, Uffz Steding, was killed, but the wireless operator, Gefr Schank, baled out into captivity on Manston aerodrome. As a bomber, therefore, the inclusion of this photograph of the Messerschmitt 110 shot down on Manston aerodrome is warranted within the context of this book's subject matter.

The same unit was in action again the next day, 15 August, during what should have been an attack against the RAF fighter airfield at Kenley in Surrey. Instead, the raiding force mistook RAF Croydon, a few miles to the north, as being RAF Kenley. A devastating attack against Croydon was carried out, but it was not without cost to the raiding force of Messerschmitt 110s from Erpr.Gr 210. Amongst them was this aircraft of Stab.Erpr.Gr 210, flown by the Gruppe Technical Officer, Lt Carl-Heinz Koch, shot down by fighter action as it headed back towards the Sussex coast and home. His radio operator/gunner, Uffz Rolf Kahl, was hit five times by machine gun bullets and very badly wounded. Making a belly landing at School Farm in Hooe, East Sussex, both men were taken into captivity, although so serious were Kahl's wounds that he was repatriated to Germany via the Red Cross in 1943.

(*Above*) This is a close-up of the unit emblem carried on Koch's Messerschmitt and all other aircraft of the unit: a red painted map of the British Isles framed in a German gun-sight.

(*Opposite above*) To guard against the possibility of destruction from the air before it could be moved, the aircraft was later covered over with camouflage netting which has been pulled back to facilitate this and the previous photograph.

(*Opposite below*) Left behind in France was Carl-Heinz Wilhelm's pet dog 'Grock' who was named after a well-known German comedian of the 1930s. He is photographed here sitting on top of one of the 250kg bombs carried by the unit's aircraft.

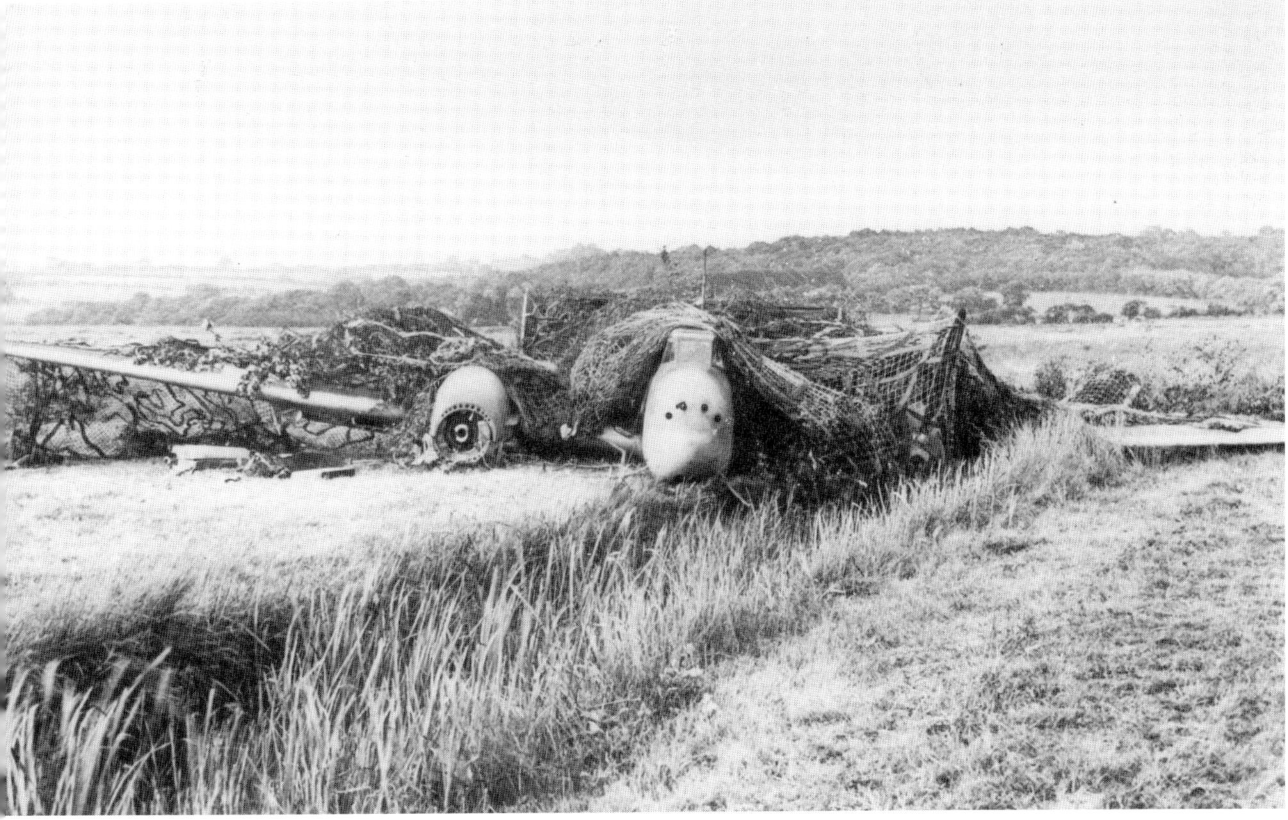

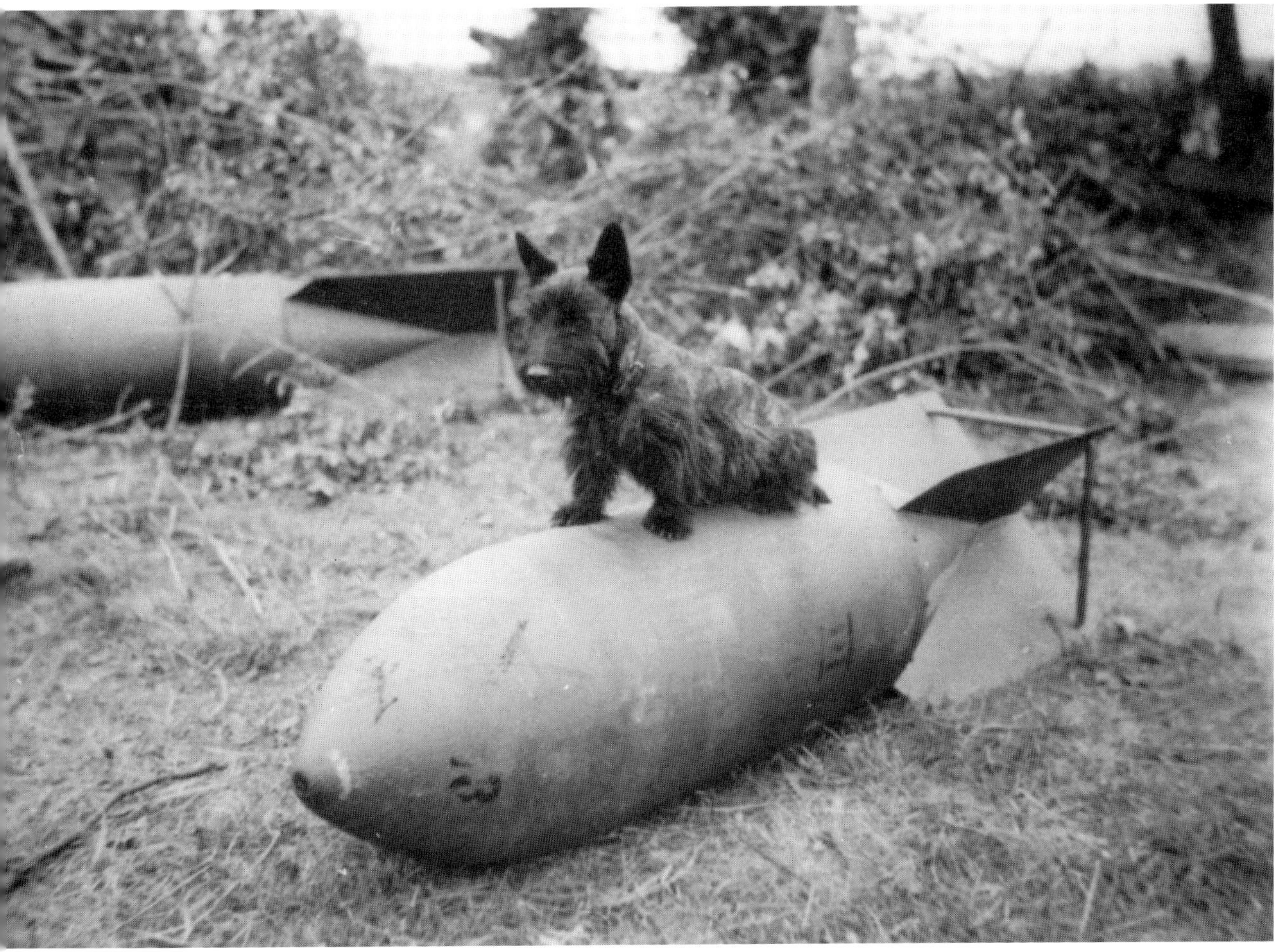

(*Left*) Also lost that day was the commander of Erprobungsgruppe 210, Hptm Walter Rubensdorffer, killed when his Messerschmitt 110 was shot down in flames at Rotherfield, East Sussex, as he headed home after mistakenly leading his unit to attack RAF Croydon.

(*Right*) Ogefr Ludwig Kretzer, Rubensdorffer's radio operator/gunner, also perished with him on 15 August 1940.

(*Opposite above*) Another Messerschmitt 110-D of Erprobungsgruppe, on another airfield and in a surprisingly similar heap of wreckage to that photographed at RAF Manston the day before. This time one of the Croydon attackers comes to grief on the aerodrome at RAF Redhill on 15 August 1940. The pilot died three days later from his severe wounds, but the radio operator/air gunner was captured unhurt.

(*Opposite below*) Although most of the Luftwaffe action against Britain during August 1940 was directed towards the southern counties, 15 August 1940 saw a noteworthy raid carried out by Junkers 88s of KG30 across the North Sea to Yorkshire, with RAF Driffield being the target. Several of the raiding force were shot down, including this aircraft of 3./KG30 which burnt itself out at Hamilton Hill Farm, Barnstown, near Bridlington. The crew of four were captured unharmed. Here, a group of soldiers guarding the wreck place themselves at some considerable personal risk by standing perhaps rather too close to the blazing bomber.

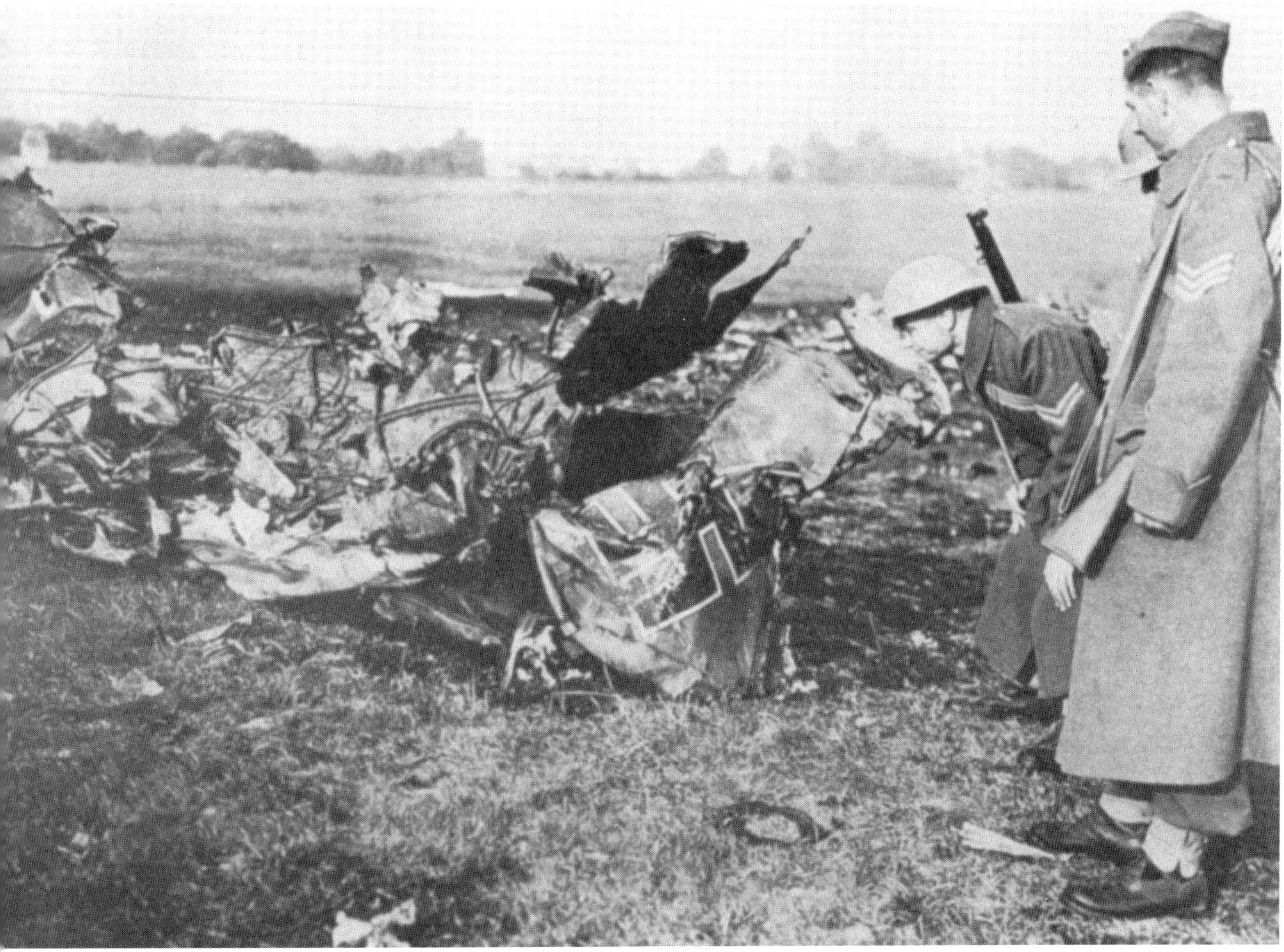

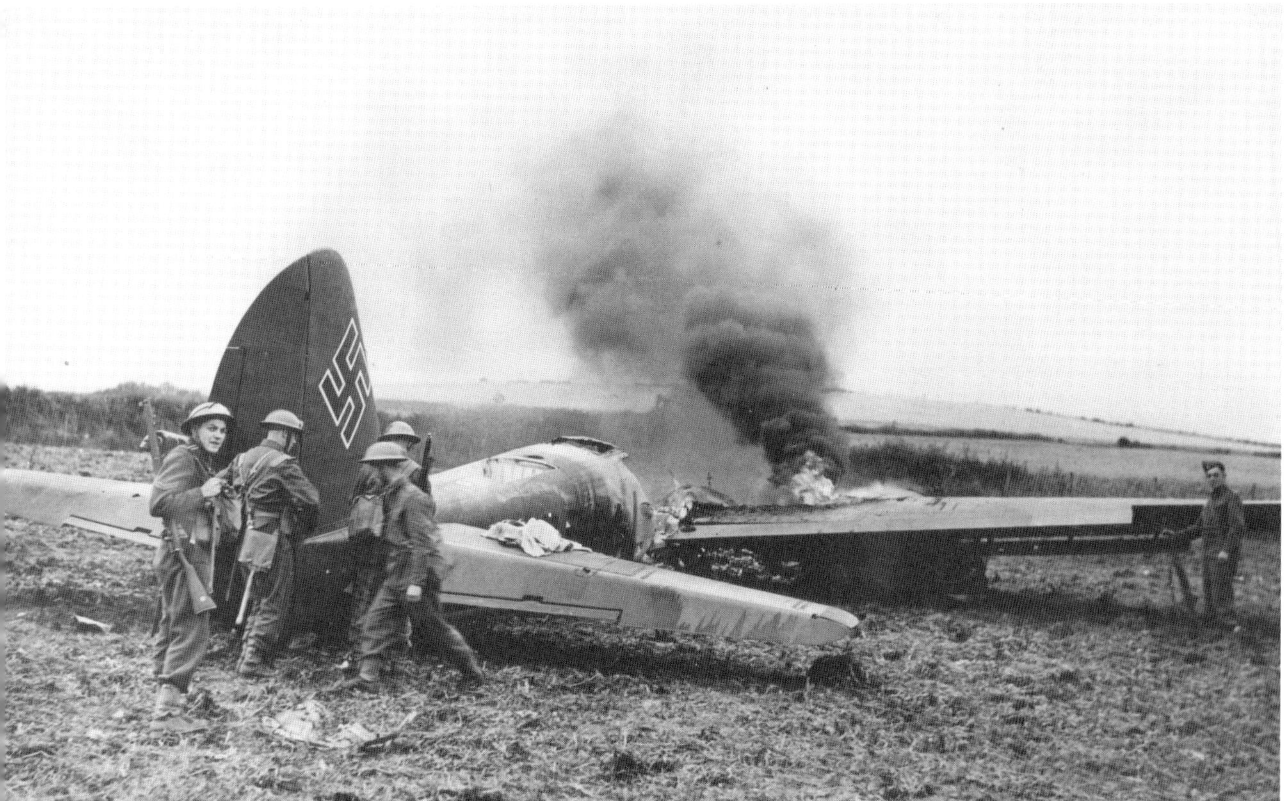

(*Above*) Another Luftwaffe loss in the north of the British Isles on 15 August 1940 was this Heinkel 115, this time operating with 1./KuFlGr.506. The seaplane flew into the ground on the Panmure Estate at Arbroath after its pilot was dazzled by searchlights while low flying. Of the crew, one was killed outright and two others were very seriously injured with one dying later in hospital. The third was so seriously injured that he was repatriated to Germany in 1943 during the Red Cross repatriation of severely wounded personnel that year and which also included another 15 August 1940 casualty, Rolf Kahl, mentioned in a preceding caption. The severed tail unit of the Heinkel 115 lies in a standing crop like some futuristic monument while a member of the local constabulary investigates.

(*Opposite above*) Back to the south of England, and the seat of most activity during the Battle of Britain. This Junkers 88 of 4./LG1 was caught over West Sussex by Hurricanes of 43 Squadron on 15 August 1940 with no less than seven pilots lining up, one after the other, to pour bullets into the bomber. Eventually, the stricken aircraft crashed and caught fire at Priors Leaze near Westbourne, West Sussex. Two of the crew were dead, the other two badly wounded. Given the relentless hail of machine gun fire that had repeatedly raked the bomber from nose to tail, and its subsequent heavy crash landing, it is somewhat surprising that anyone was able to emerge alive from the wreck.

(*Opposite below*) Friday, 16 August 1940 was another heavily fought day for the Luftwaffe, and another day of very heavy losses. This was all that was left of a Heinkel 111 of 4./KG55 that exploded violently with its bomb load at Upper Frithfold Farm, Northchapel, West Sussex, after an engagement with a Hurricane of 1 Squadron. None of the crew was able to escape the doomed bomber, which lost the outboard of one wing as it was sent flaming into the ground. The tremendous explosion blasted a crater which remains as a pond to this day. Of the crew, only one could be identified: the pilot, Fw Ernst Müller.

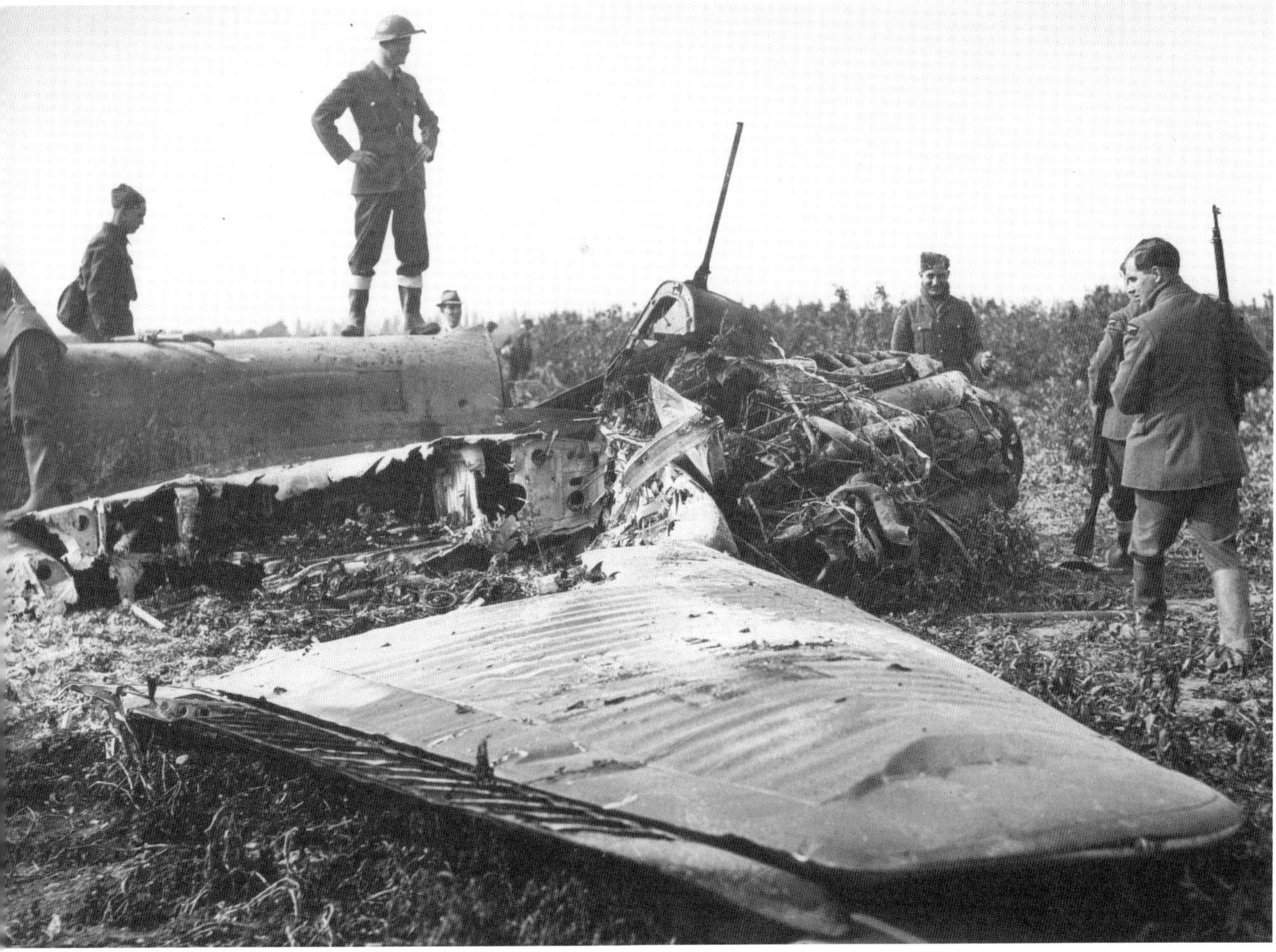

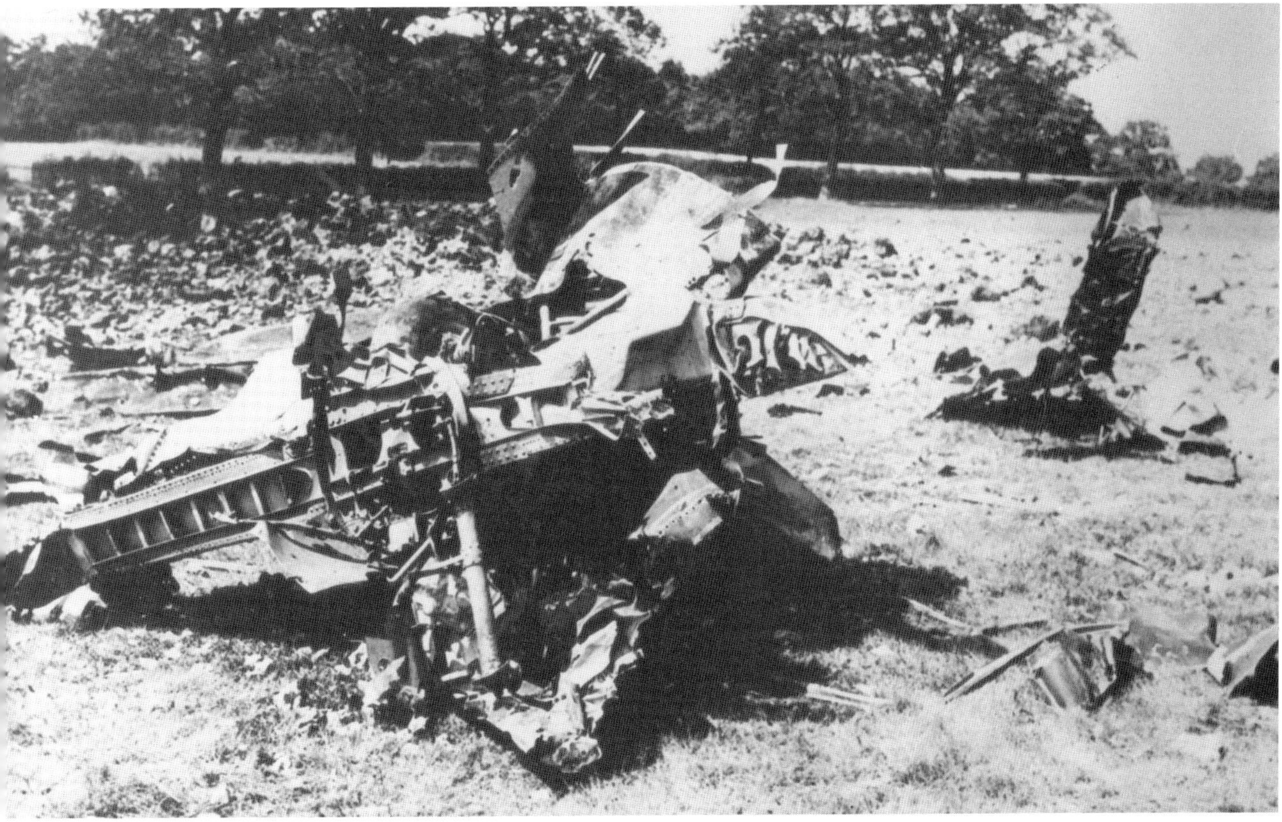

(*Above*) Ernst Müller was the only one of the five airmen who could be named on the white cross marker when the crew were buried in this collective grave at Ebernoe Churchyard, West Sussex. Subsequently, the airmen have been exhumed for re-burial at the German Military Cemetery, Cannock Chase, where they have now all been given named graves and headstones.

(*Opposite above*) Kampfgeschwader 55 had a bad day over Sussex on 16 August 1940, losing another two aircraft over the county during late afternoon air operations. This aircraft of 6./KG55 was brought down by fighter action and crash landed at Annington Farm, Bramber, after sustaining damage to its oil system in attacks by Hurricanes of 1 and 615 Squadron. The damage caused engine failure and the pilot had no choice but to land. The aircraft was en route to bomb Heathrow and sixteen 50kg bombs were found in the fuselage that had to be dealt with before the aircraft could be removed.

(*Opposite below*) Not far away, at Honeysuckle Lane in High Salvington, just to the north of Worthing, this 7./KG55 Heinkel 111 was shot down by Spitfires of 602 Squadron who continued firing at the stricken bomber until it had touched down. Two of the five crew had been killed, and another seriously wounded. RAF Intelligence Officers investigating the wreck found 300 to 400 bullet holes in the aircraft and the evidence of this onslaught is clearly evident here. A German-speaking civilian, one of the first on the scene, was talking to the crew when the Police and military arrived and was arrested as a suspected spy. He was not released from his cell at Worthing Police Station for some hours, and until his identity and *bone-fide* status could be established.

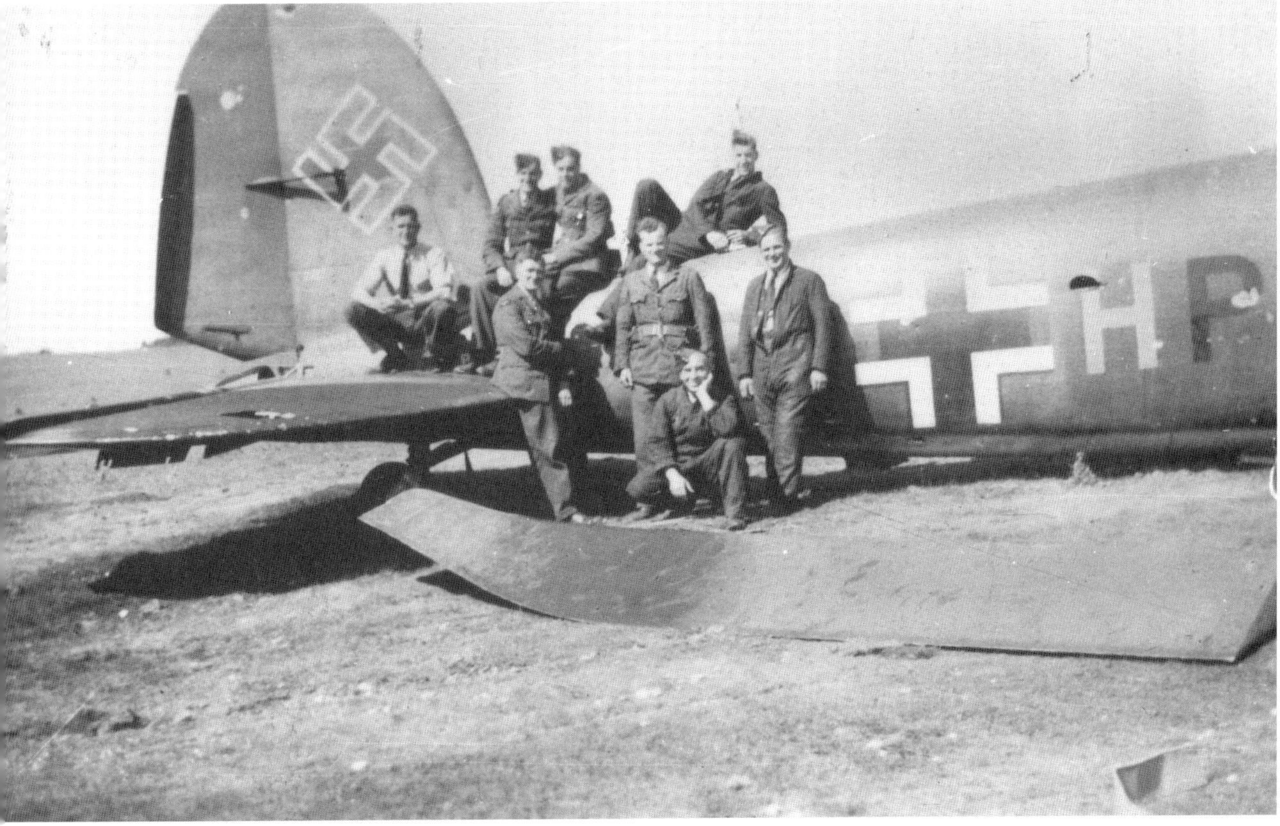

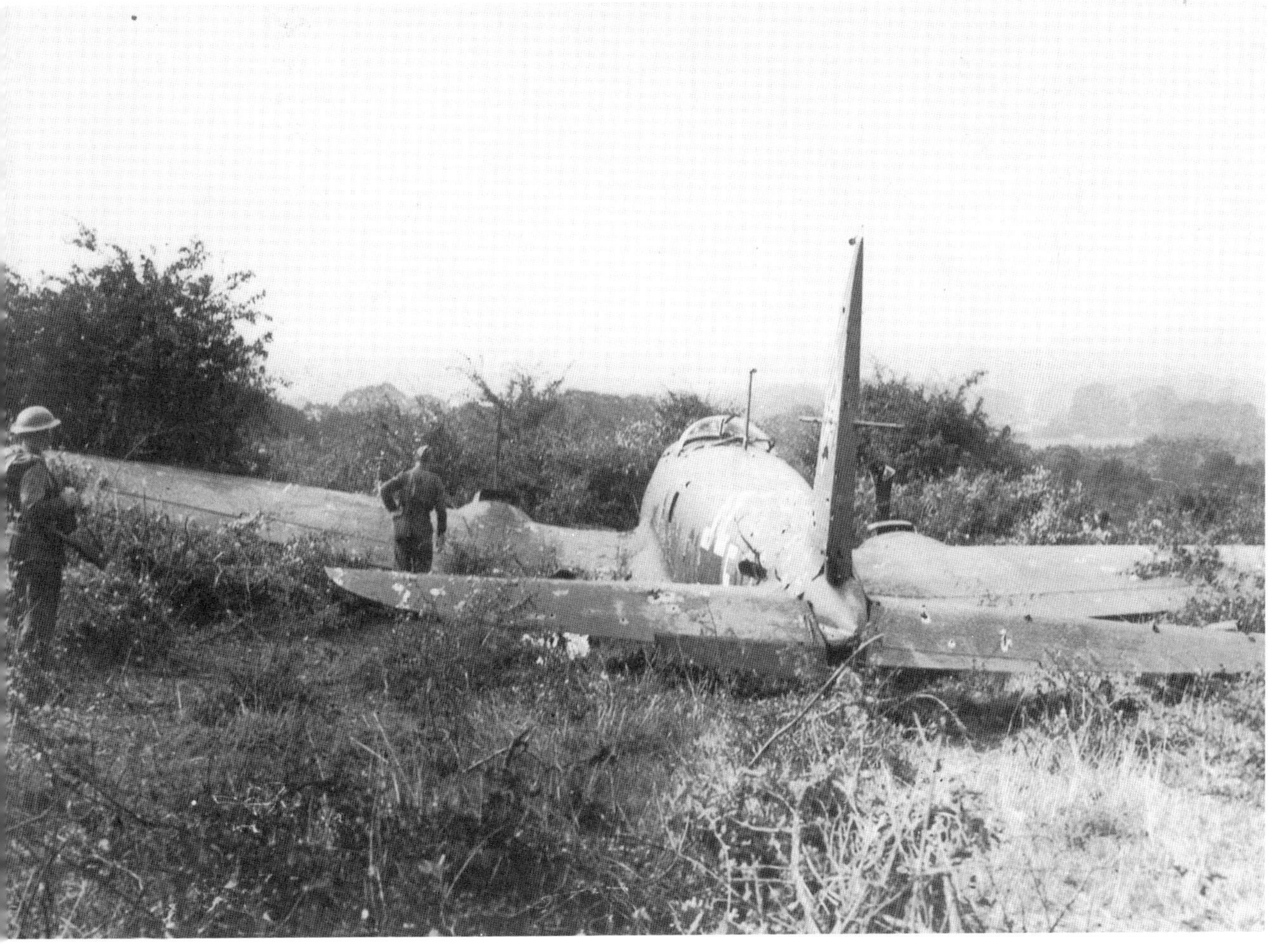

(*Above*) Apart from the Luftwaffe casualties, this rabbit had the misfortune to be struck by the bomber as it made its crash landing. It must have been the unluckiest rabbit in England. Getting run over by vehicles on Honeysuckle Lane was perhaps a daily hazard, but the odds against getting run down by a crashing Heinkel on its own patch of countryside must have been very considerable indeed!

(*Opposite above*) Another example of the official censor striking out parts of a photograph that he felt to be militarily sensitive. In this photograph he has used white rectangles to block out the code letters on the fuselage which give away the identity of the unit to which this aircraft belonged.

(*Opposite below*) From 13 August until early September 1940 the Luftwaffe concentrated most of its effort on attacking airfields, radar stations and other sites connected to the aviation industry. On 16 August 1940 a particularly heavy raid was directed at RAF Tangmere in West Sussex by Junkers 87 Stuka dive-bombers. From Colworth, near Bognor Regis, press photographer Frank Lalouette captured this column of oily black smoke rising in the distance from Tangmere airfield. Because of the military sensitivity associated with such photographs it was unsurprisingly never approved by the official censor for wartime publication.

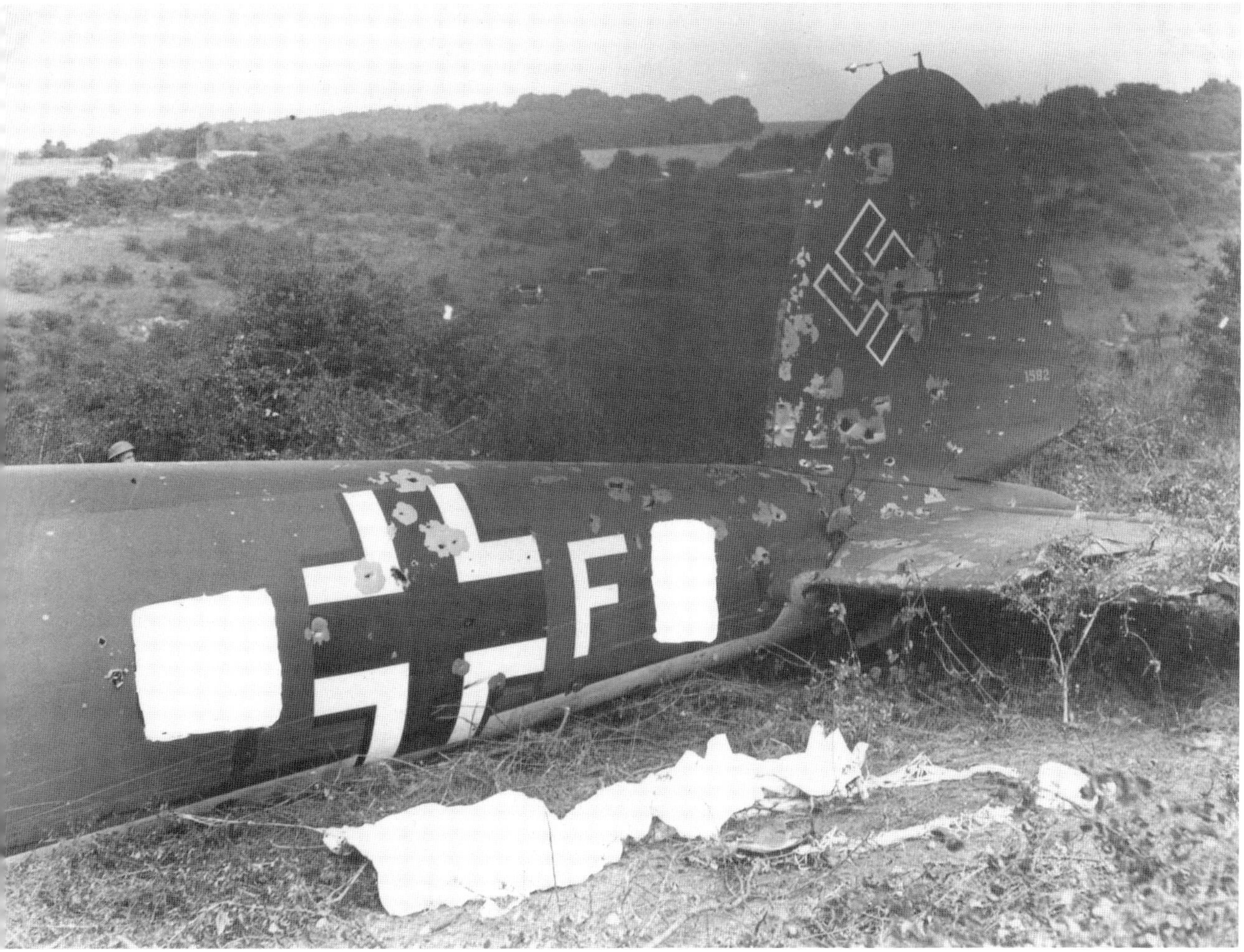
F

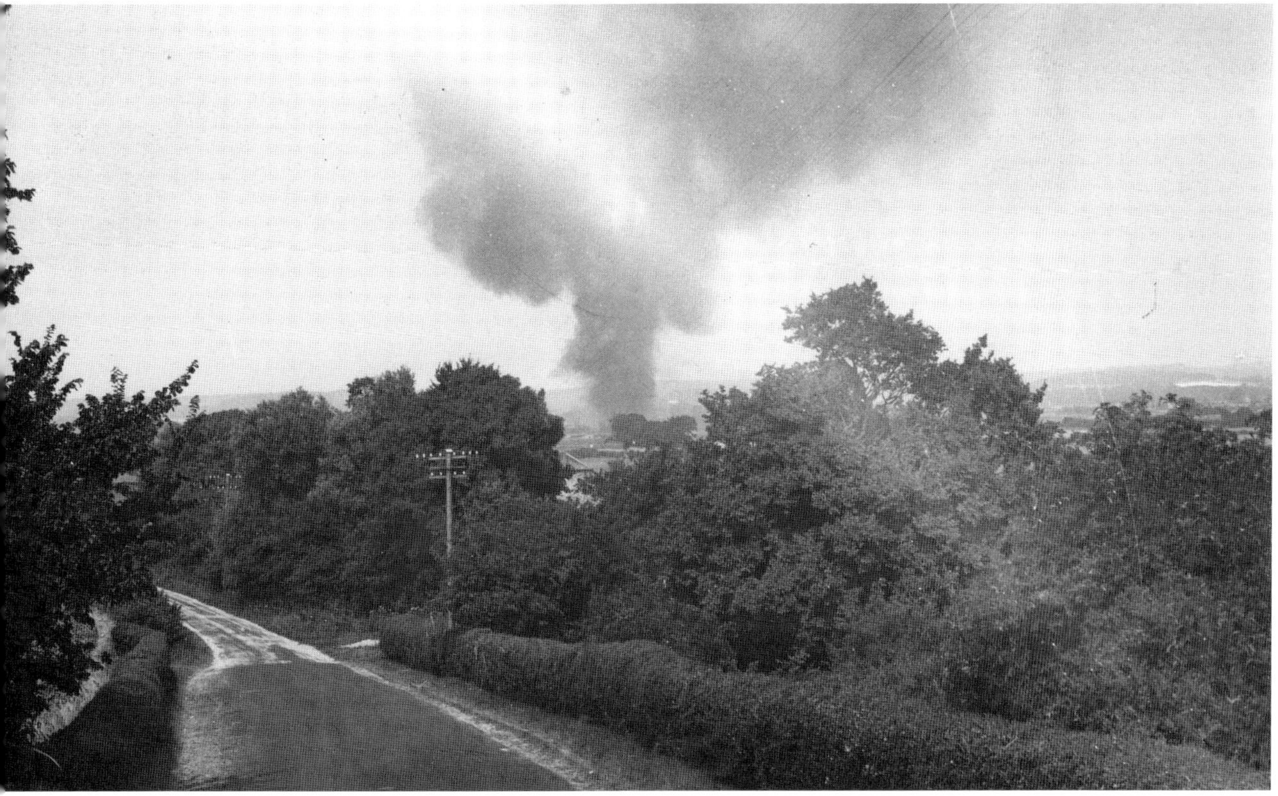

Some of the photographs taken by Lalouette of the Junkers 87 raiders downed after the Tangmere raid were passed for publication. At Bowley Farm, South Mundham, Frank captured these shots of a battered Stuka of 3./StG2 that had been shot down moments after bombing Tangmere. Pursued by a Hurricane of 601 Squadron, the bullet-holed Stuka crashed through trees before coming to rest in this rather battered condition. Both crew had been hit in the head by bullets, killing the radio operator/gunner instantly and grievously wounding the pilot. Despite his injuries, the pilot managed a creditable landing but died in hospital the next day.

Rather less intact was another Stuka of 3./StG2 which ploughed into the ground at Honor Farm, Pagham, that day. The aircraft totally disintegrated, killing its pilot Uffz Paul Linse (inset) and Ogefr Rudolf Messerschmidt.

A soldier examines a shattered piece of the crashed Stuka's wing at Honor Farm that bears the remnants of one of the crosses. Little else that was recognisable survived the ferocity of the crash or the subsequent fire and explosion.

This Stuka of 3./StG2 and its crew fared rather better than some of the others brought down after the raid on Tangmere of 16 August 1940. Shot down by fighters, the aircraft careered across the Church Norton to Selsey Road before coming to a halt in a roadside hedge. On its bumpy passage across fields, a road, a pavement and then through a hedge, the undercarriage legs were torn off before the Stuka finally ground to a halt. Both crew members were wounded, but taken POW. Bizarrely, it was reported that the radio operator/air gunner had an American Stars & Stripes flag in his possession when taken into captivity.

Perhaps because of the failure of the intended raid on RAF Kenley on 15 August 1940 another mission was ordered, this time to be carried out by a specialist low-level attack unit, the Dornier 17-Z-equipped 9./KG76. Nine of the unit's aircraft streaked low across the English Channel at lunchtime on 18 August, just above the waves, crossing the Sussex coast at Cuckmere Haven. Here, the aircraft are photographed passing Beachy Head and its famous lighthouse. An Observer Corps post on top of the cliffs spotted the raiders who were tracked all the way to their target.

Moments later and Cuckmere Haven and Seaford Head are ahead. This photograph catches the view through the ring-and-bead crosshairs of one the Dornier's forward firing machine guns.

Crossing the coast, Seaford is just off to port. How low this flight was can be judged by the shadow of the Dornier that can be seen flitting across the fields only about 60 feet below the bomber.

Next, the railway line from Newhaven to Lewes is crossed with Southease Railway Station and the nearby cement works in clear view.

(*Above*) The Dorniers turned at Burgess Hill onto a track heading the formation due north, and directly towards RAF Kenley. In this photograph, people in Cyprus Road run for cover as the war photographer on board one of the raiders records a brief moment in the history of the Battle of Britain. Simultaneously, the formation of nine aircraft was machine gunning streets, buildings and vehicles en route to their target.

(*Above*) The raiding force, however, suffered grievous losses in the raid with anti-aircraft fire, a rocket-launched parachute and cable defensive 'curtain', and defending RAF fighters all taking a very heavy toll on the attackers. Here, just outside the northern boundary of RAF Kenley, the shattered remains of one the Dorniers lays strewn around a field beyond the garden of a house in Golf Road as a pig grubs contentedly around the wreckage. All five crew members were killed in the crash. Only a few minutes earlier the same aircrew were confidently passing Beachy Head on their fast and low run-in to target.

(*Opposite below*) Roaring in at little more than hangar-height across the southern edge of RAF Kenley, the nine Dorniers each unleashed their cargo of twenty 50kg bombs and raked the aerodrome with cannon and machine gun fire. Passing the northern edge of the airfield, smoke puffs are thrown up by the attacker's gunfire around the fighter dispersal pens where a Spitfire of 64 Squadron sits impotently in its protective revetment. Considerable damage and destruction was caused to hangars and airfield buildings, with a number of fatalities and injuries among service personnel. A number of aircraft were also destroyed or damaged on the ground.

(*Left*) Fw Karl Greulich was one of that confident band of aviators who had hedge-hopped across Sussex and Surrey to Kenley that day. He was one of the five crew members killed in the Golf Road crash.

(*Below*) The crashing Dornier had fallen onto a house called 'Sunnycroft', completely demolishing it, and resulting in a remarkably lucky escape by its occupant, a Mr Turner-Smith.

Another of the Kenley raiders crashed in flames at Leaves Green, close to RAF Biggin Hill, with all five crew members injured. In total, four of the Dornier 17s were shot down over land or fell into the English Channel, and others made crash landings or emergency landings back in France with wounded, dead or dying crew members on board. Only one Dornier 17 returned to its home base at Cormeilles-en-Vexin. The cost to 9./KG76 had been high, and RAF Kenley remained operational.

On 18 August 1940, the hardest fought day of the Battle of Britain, the Junkers 87 Stuka dive-bombers again returned to the assault on England. As with the casualties sustained by the Dorniers of 9./KG76 that same day, the Stuka losses would also strike a serious blow to the Luftwaffe. One of the targets, though, the Fleet Air Arm station at Ford in West Sussex, took a heavy casualty toll, and buildings and aircraft were left wrecked and burning.

A further scene of the devastation at Ford where many of the wooden hutted accommodation buildings were blasted to matchwood. Other airfields and RAF targets along the Sussex and Hampshire coastline were also subjected to Stuka attack that day.

One of the most enduring images of the Battle of Britain shows this death-dive of a 3./StG77 Junkers 87 Stuka high above the rooftops of Chichester on 18 August 1940, shot down on its approach to dive-bomb nearby RAF Thorney Island. Although they were possibly already dead or disabled at their stations, both crew members perished when their aircraft finally crashed at The Broyle on the outskirts of the city.

This was the aftermath of the Stuka's impact, as an oily black column of smoke coiled skywards from the funeral pyre of shattered wreckage.

(*Above*) Another of the RAF Thorney raiders from StG77 was shot down at the same time, its crew being more fortunate than their comrades in the Broyle crash when they baled out into captivity leaving their Stuka to plummet into Chichester Harbour at Fishbourne Creek. Here, Oblt Johannes Wilhelm waits at Chichester Station for a train ride to his interrogation in London and an eventual POW camp. A kindly British soldier hands Wilhelm a cigarette with a passing commuter throwing a curious glance while another civilian at the end of the bench is a study in indifference. Johannes Wilhelm was covered in oil from his Stuka's crippled engine when he baled out, with the dark oil stains on his shirt collar telling their own story.

(*Opposite page*) Although the Junkers 86-P is not an aircraft generally associated with Luftwaffe air activity over Britain, they were used in limited numbers in the high-altitude reconnaissance role. Teenager Alexander McKee took a photograph of a single extremely high vapour trail over Portsmouth at around 1.30pm on 18 August 1940 and this was almost certainly the trail left by a Junkers 86-P as it went about its work.

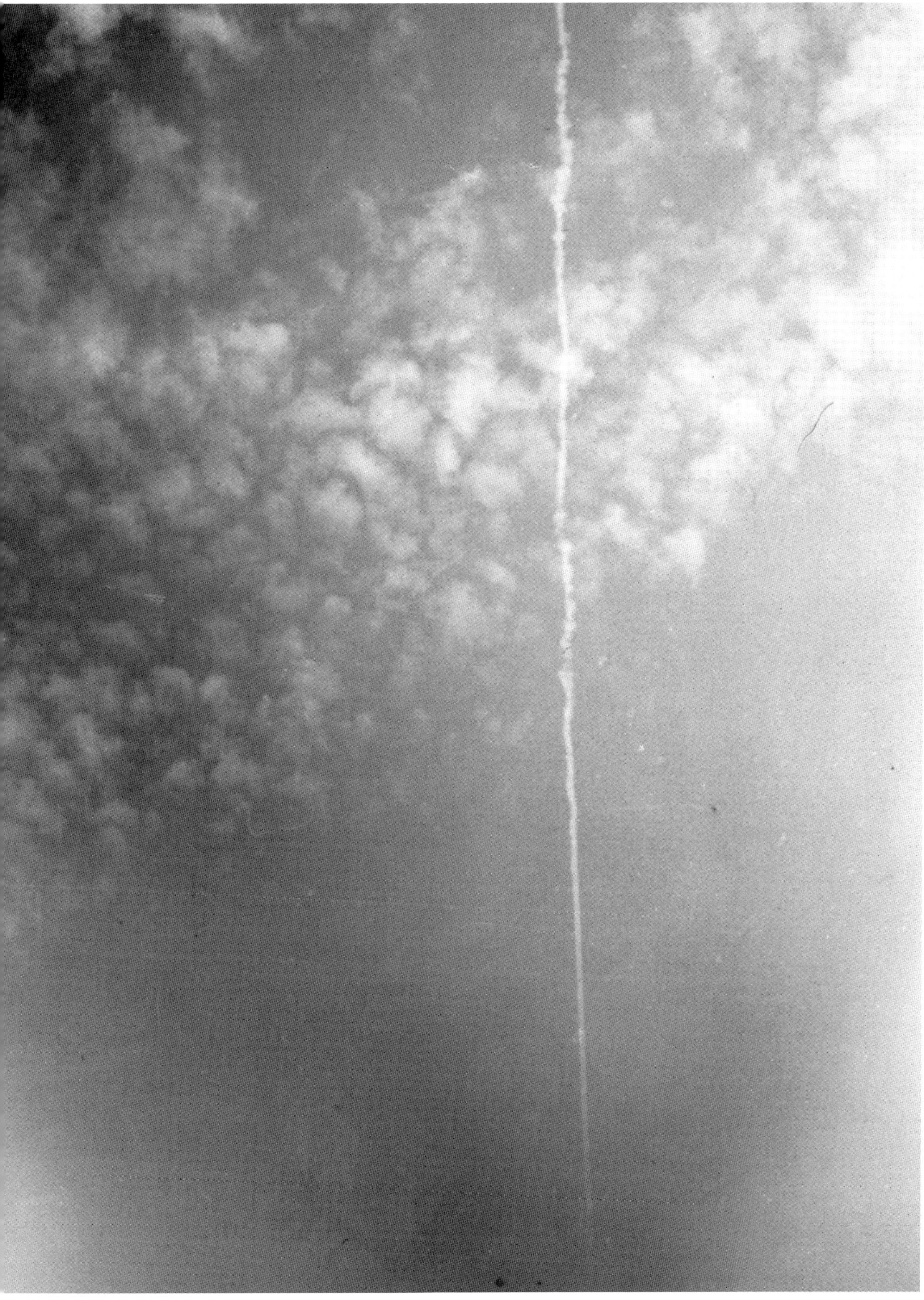

(*Above*) The Junkers 86-P was powered by double-supercharged diesel engines and had a pressurised cabin for the crew. None were ever brought down over the British Isles, although on 18 August 1940 one of these aircraft carried out a high altitude photographic reconnaissance run over the various targets attacked along the south coast by the Luftwaffe that day.

(*Opposite above*) After a relative lull in Luftwaffe activity over Britain on 19 August 1940, the next day saw some limited sorties, including three Junkers 88s of 8./KG30 which made the long crossing of the North Sea from Aalborg, Denmark, to attack airfields and harbours in the area of Hull. After finding landfall, this aircraft was attacked by three Hurricanes. The pilot managed to lose them for a while in clouds, but when he emerged, the Hurricanes were still with him. Successive attacks wounded the wireless operator and gunner and set fire to the cockpit. As a result, the pilot decided to land to seek first aid for his wounded crew and eventually got the bomber down at Patrington, Yorkshire. Both wounded men died in hospital, one the next day and the other on 22 August 1940.

(*Opposite below*) The next day, 21 August 1940, saw a number of scattered raids across Britain, mostly carried out by single aircraft. Still maintaining the Luftwaffe's tactic of going for RAF airfields, a Dornier 17-Z of 8./KG2 was shot down through the combined efforts of fighters and anti-aircraft guns whilst heading for RAF Wyton, and crashed at Gippeswyk Park at Ipswich in Suffolk after the crew, two of them injured, had abandoned the bomber and parachuted into captivity. Firemen and a soldier pick through the smouldering remnants.

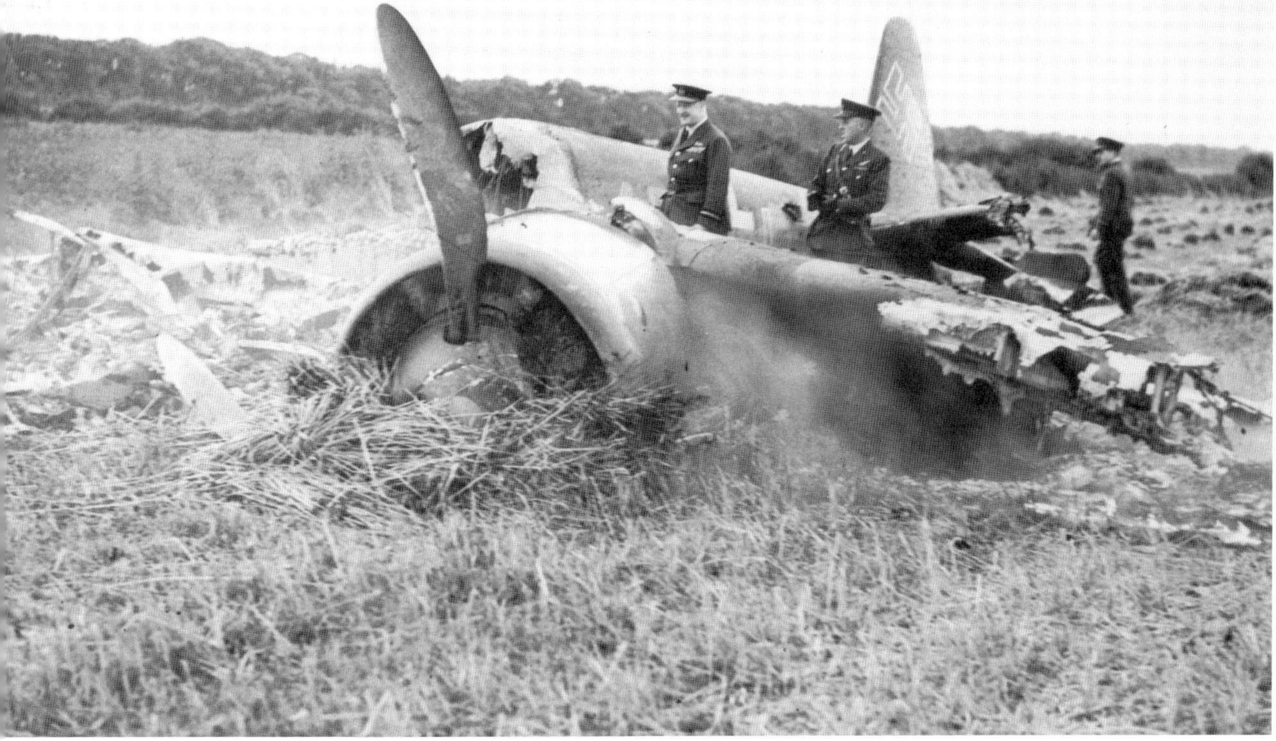

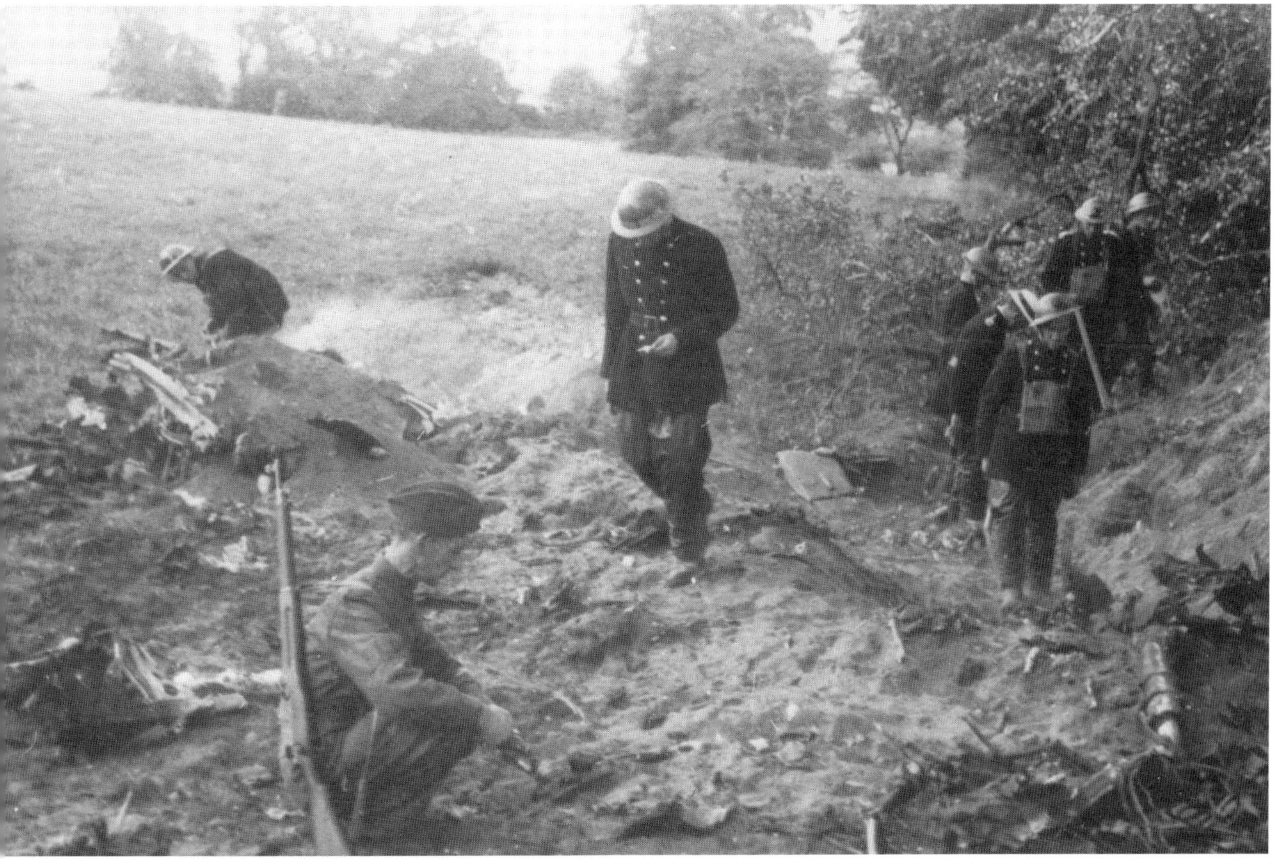

Off Scolt Head, Brancaster, Norfolk, a Dornier 17-Z of 4./KG3 was shot down on 21 August 1940, probably by Spitfires of 611 Squadron. All four crew were killed and two of their bodies were washed ashore at Brancaster on 23 and 24 August and were buried with full military honours by the RAF at St Margaret's Church, Catton, near Norwich. This series of five photographs show the honour accorded the foe in their burial, which includes an RAF padre, a bearer and escort party, coffins draped with Swastika flags and a salute fired over the graves. In one of the photographs, inquisitive locals may be seen being kept at a distance even though the ladies seem to be respectfully attired in coats and hats with the gentlemen bare-headed, with hats in their hands.

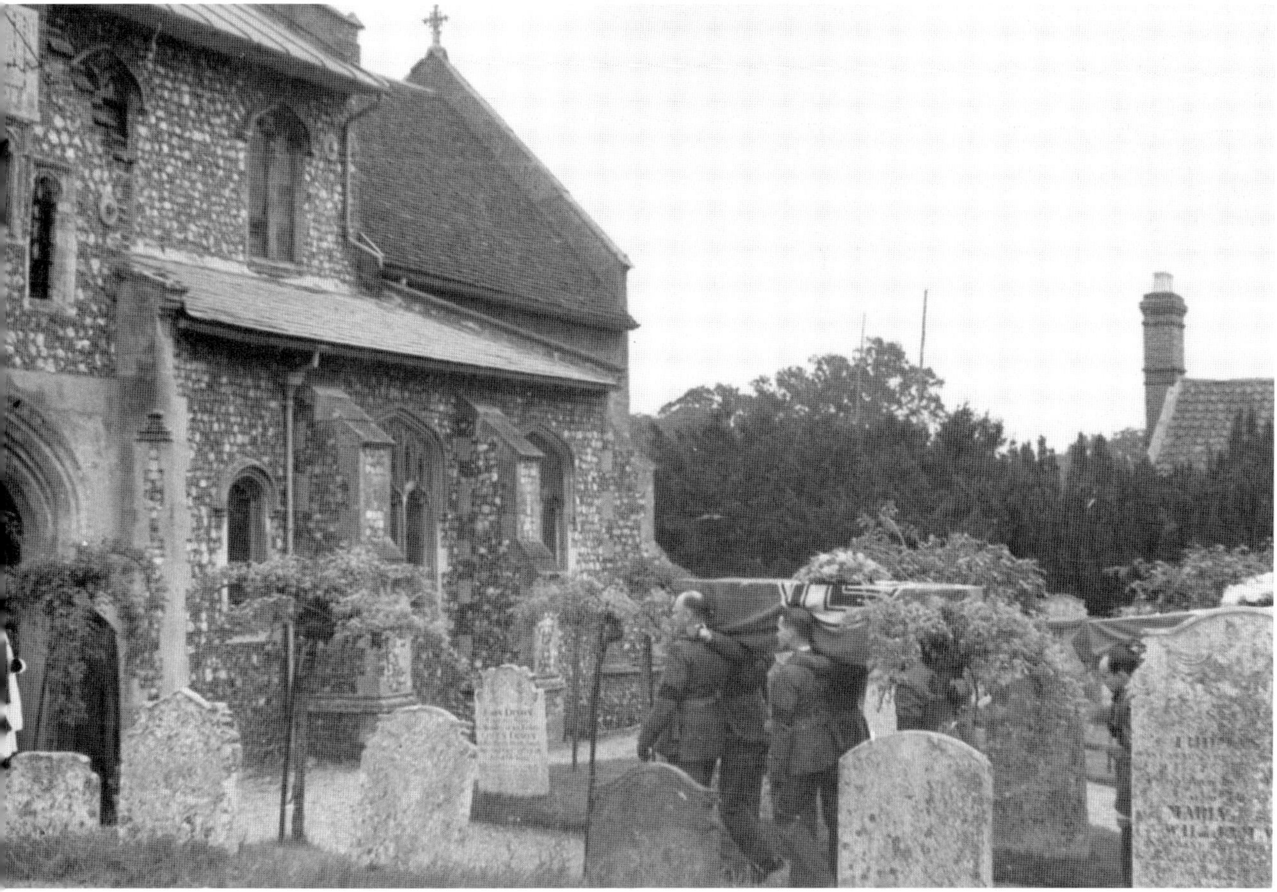

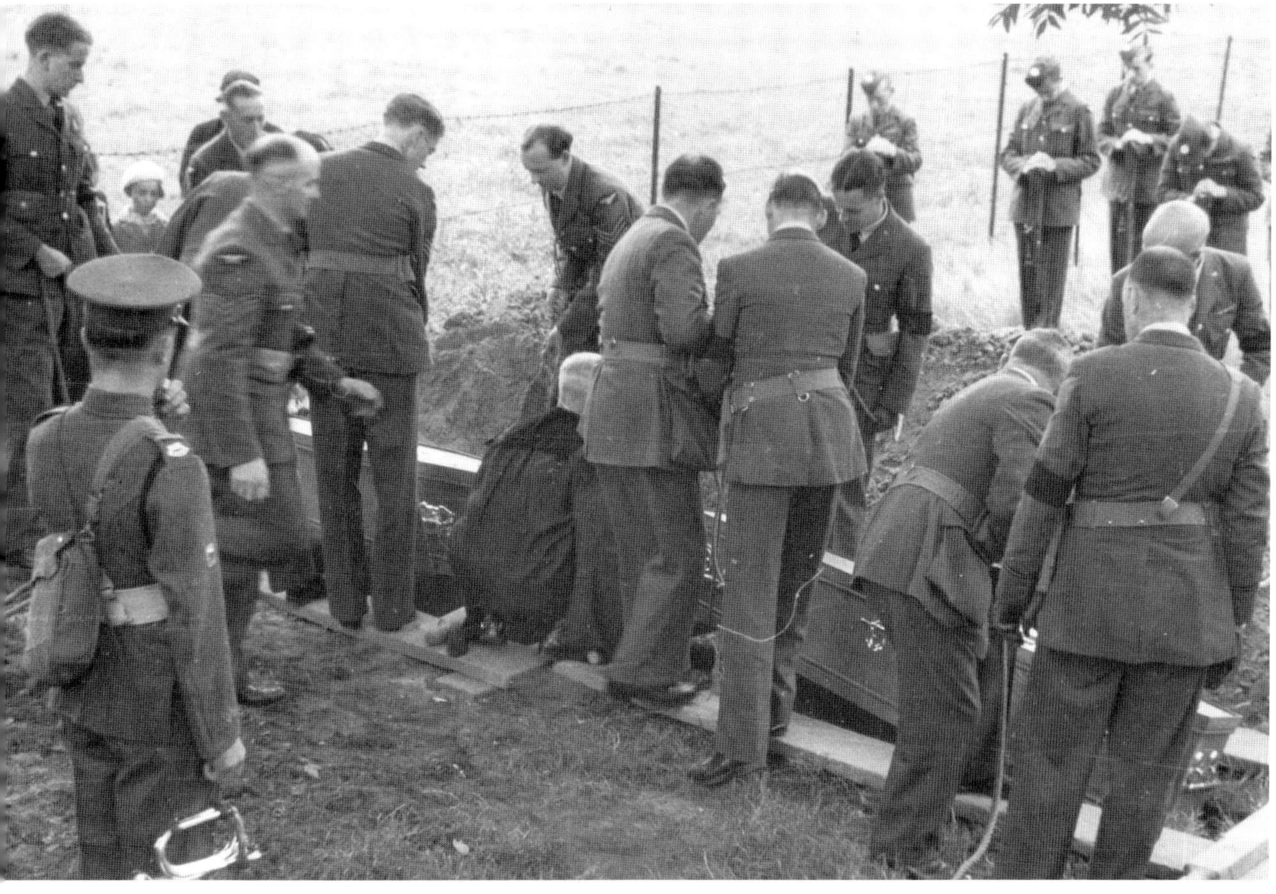

(*Below*) There was to be no grave, though, for the crew of a Junkers 88 of 1./KG54 that was shot down on Manor Farm at King's Somborne, Hampshire, by Spitfires of 234 Squadron on 21 August. The aircraft disintegrated and burnt on impact, and although human remains were said to have been removed from the site shortly after the crash no grave location for them has ever been traced. There was post-war opposition to suggestions that a memorial to the four airmen be erected in the village, a stance that seems to be in striking contrast to the turn-out of civilians at Catton (*above*) for the burial of German airmen lost the very same day.

One of the crew of the Junkers 88 shot down at King's Somborne, Gefr Franz Becker, was a champion swimmer and for many years his family had been distressed by the thought that he had perhaps gone down in the English Channel, swum until exhausted and then drowned. They were comforted by knowledge imparted to them by the author during the 1980s that the end for Franz and his four colleagues had been mercifully swift.

(*Above*) Another Junkers 88 of KG54, this time from the 4th Staffel, was hit by fighters and anti-aircraft fire on 21 August whilst en route to bomb RAF Brize Norton. All four crew escaped with their lives when the pilot made a forced landing on flat open farmland at Marsh Farm, Earnley, West Sussex, and were taken into captivity unharmed. Soldiers look at bullet holes in the tail of the Junkers.

(*Opposite above*) Here, the captain of the aircraft brought down at Marsh Farm, Hptm Lothar Mainwald, is marched off to a POW camp with his pilot, Ofw Heinz Apollony, walking closely behind him. In Luftwaffe air crews the pilot was not always the captain. This position was often held by an officer (acting as observer) with an NCO as pilot, as in this instance.

(*Opposite below*) Until the summer of 2013, when the Royal Air Force Museum, Hendon, raised a Battle of Britain Dornier 17-Z from the English Channel, this particular Dornier 17-Z may well have been the last intact surviving aircraft of its type anywhere in the world. Shot down during an attack on RAF Rochford on 26 August 1940, this machine was shot down by RAF fighters and actually ended up making a crash landing on the very aerodrome it was attacking. All four of the crew were captured, albeit wounded. The aircraft was sent to the Royal Aircraft Establishment at Farnborough for examination and was subsequently dismantled, crated and stored. It is then believed that it remained in storage until 1950 when it was scrapped.

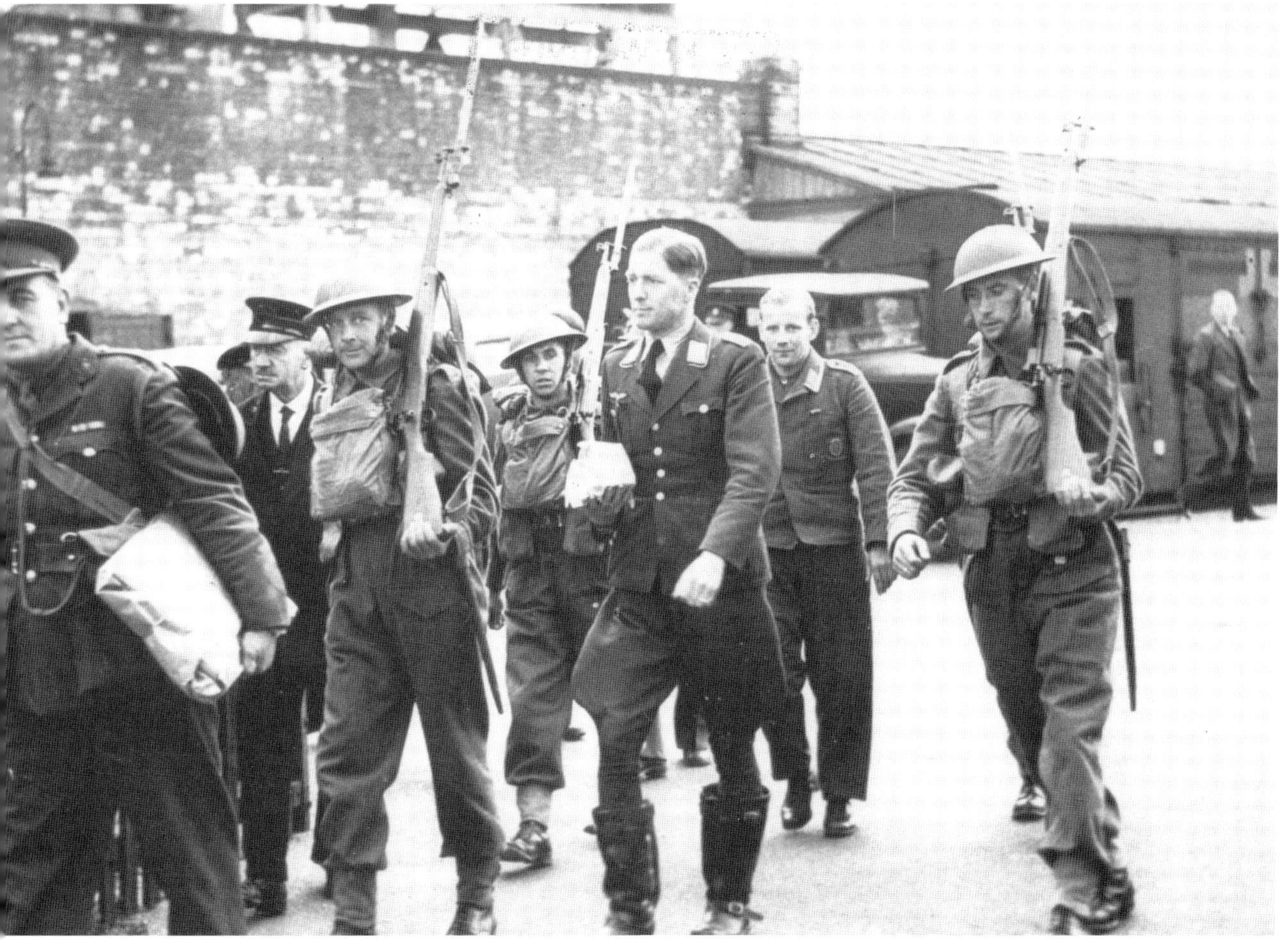

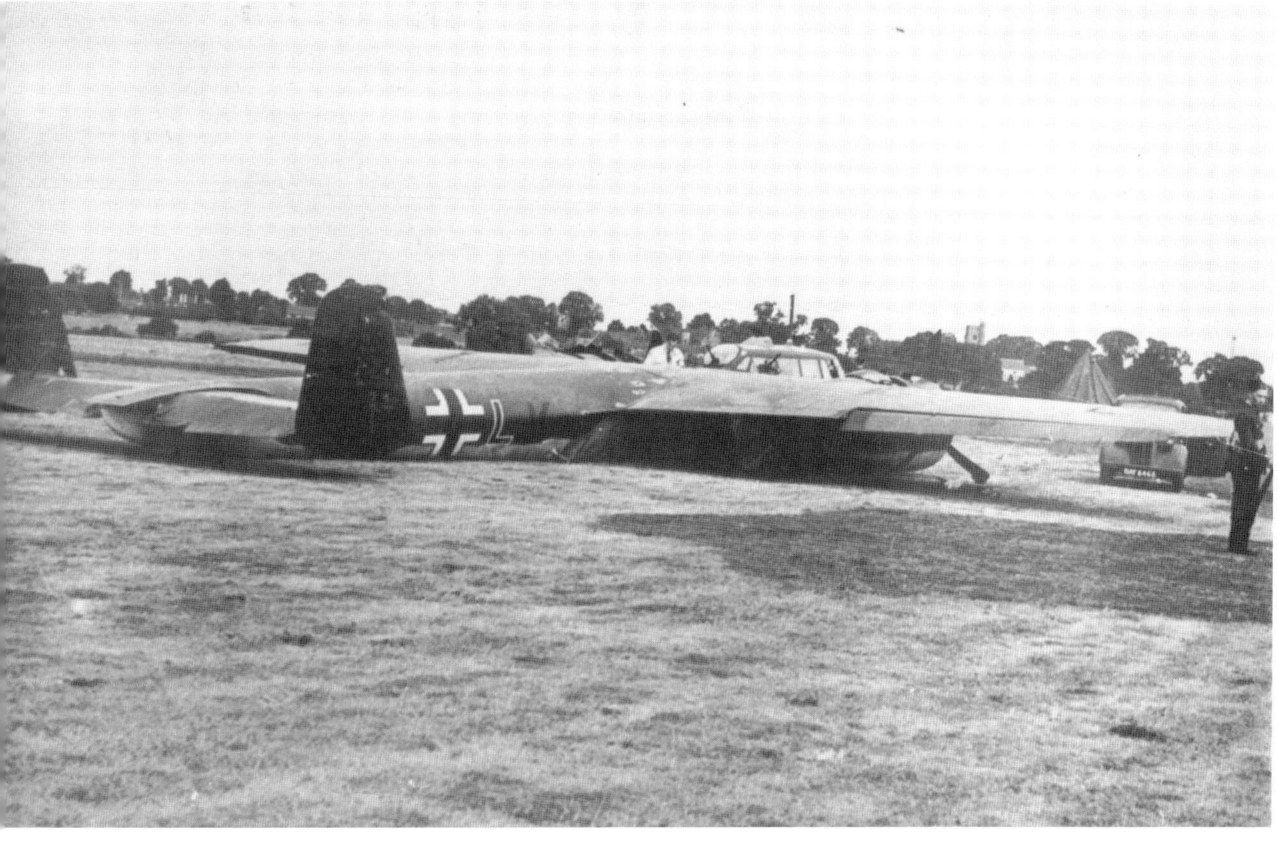

(*Above*) The same day, another Dornier 17-Z of the same unit was shot down during an attack on RAF Hornchurch. On the return flight, both engines were hit and put out of action and the pilot made a good belly landing two miles south-west of RAF Eastchurch on the Isle of Sheppey in Kent. Three crew members were captured, but the captain and observer, Oblt Siegfried Hertel, was killed.

(*Right & opposite page*) A photographer captured the interior and exterior of the cockpit, showing the bristling array of defensive 7.92mm MG15 machine guns. A 20mm cannon for ground-attack was also fixed in the nose, forward firing.

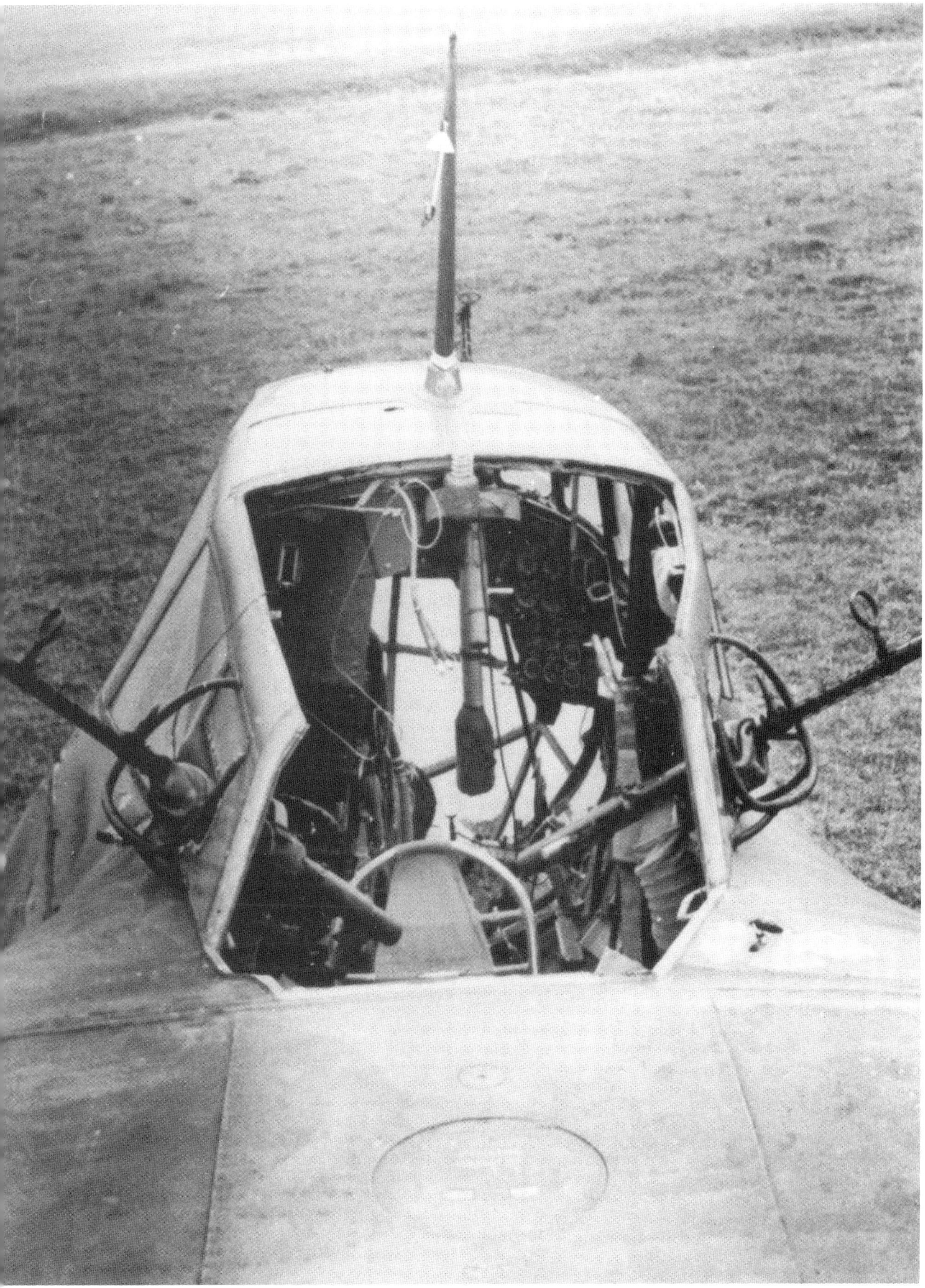

(*Above*) Photographed with their Dornier 17-Z shortly before their final mission on 26 August 1940 are (from left to right) the pilot, Uffz Ambros Schmelzer, the captain, Oblt Siegfried Hertel and the radio operator, Uffz Helmuth Buhr.

(*Opposite above*) On the same day another Dornier 17-Z of KG2, this time from the 7th Staffel, was one of three aircraft from that unit that bombed RAF Debden. The formation was intercepted on the way into the target, and again on the way out. Separated from the rest of the formation and losing oil from one engine, the navigator was badly wounded and it became obvious that his condition was such that he would not be able to bale out. Two other crew members were also wounded and the pilot reported that the aircraft would not be able to make the return journey to its base at Cambrai and was rapidly losing altitude. Despite his injuries, Uffz Frederick Knorky made a good forced landing at Whepstead, near Bury St Edmunds, although the navigator, Uffz Heinrich Schäffer, died of his wounds on 22 September 1940. In its landing run, the Dornier stopped just short of a stone wall where the emerging crew were immediately confronted by a young lady on a horse and wielding a shotgun. RAF investigators found a bloodstained sketch map in the cockpit showing where the crew's two sticks of bombs had fallen on RAF Debden: one row across buildings and another line between two hangars.

(*Opposite below*) On 30 August 1940, and with attacks on RAF aerodromes still very much the Luftwaffe's primary objective, a force of Heinkel 111s were despatched to attack the Royal Aircraft Establishment HQ at Farnborough in Hampshire. One of these bombers, of 5./KG1, became separated from the main formation by fighter attack and was then attacked by Hurricanes of 79 Squadron when nearing the target. During this attack, one of the Hurricanes collided with the Heinkel causing both aircraft to crash a short distance from each other. The RAF pilot baled out safely but the Heinkel and its bomb load exploded on impact at Swires Farm, Newdigate, Surrey, and left very little of any substance apart from this chunk of rear fuselage section with its tail wheel still attached. Although three of the crew were killed, two baled out and became Prisoners of War. One of these was Hptm R. Bäss who features in the photograph on page 88.

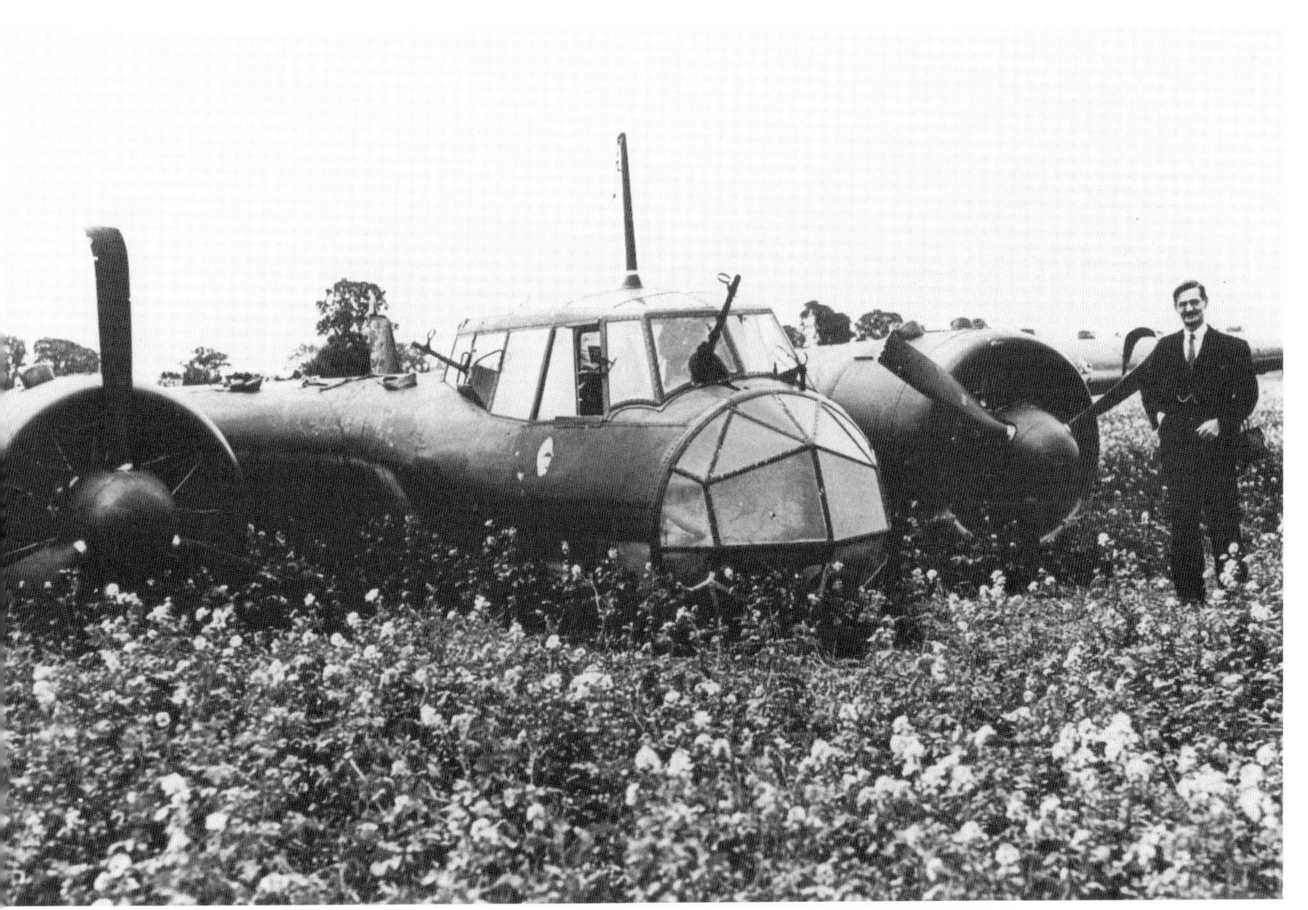

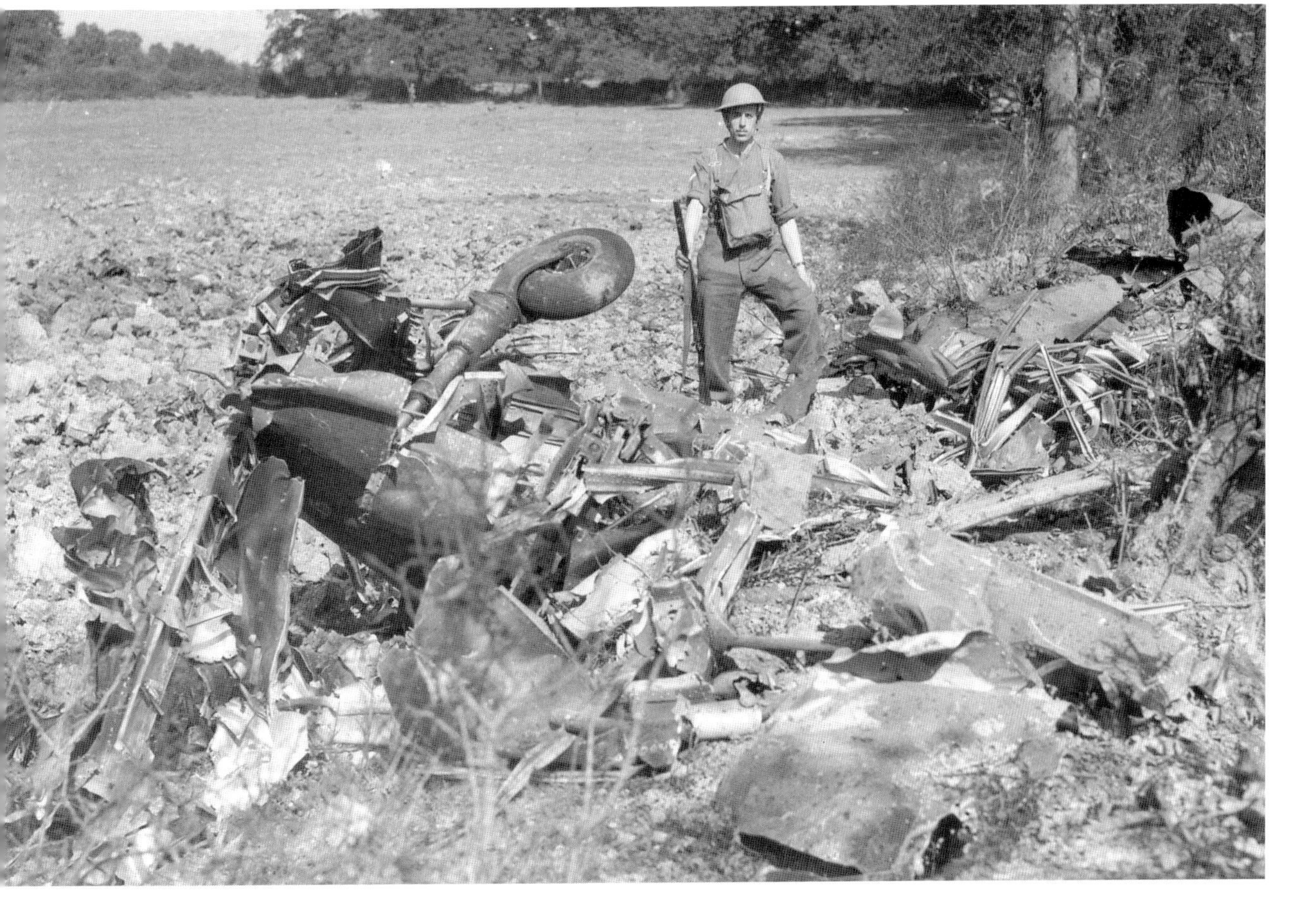

Ogefr. Raths Arno
8./K.G.55

aus Aachen
geb. 4.10.20
gef. am 30.8.40
beim Flugzug gegen England

(*Above*) Another of the Farnborough raiders that day came to earth not many miles away at Haxted, near Lingfield. This time, it was a Heinkel 111 of 5./KG1 and although the crew successfully bombed their target they were then intercepted by a Hurricane of 253 Squadron flown by Plt Off J.P.B. Greenwood, whose bullets killed the gunner, Gefr Walter Reis, damaged both engines and started a small fire. Too severely damaged to make it back to France, Fw Heinz Schnabel made a good forced landing, and although one other crew member was wounded, all apart from Reis was captured. Several .303 bullet strikes were found in the oil radiators, and in this image oil can be seen to have been thrown up around the engine and propeller. Later, this Heinkel was put on display at 'Summerfields' in Hastings to raise money for the local Spitfire fund. En route to the exhibition the aircraft on its low-loader became very firmly wedged in a narrow sunken road at Powdermill Lane, Battle, East Sussex, and had to be dug free after the inboard wing stubs jammed themselves into the roadside embankments!

(*Opposite page*) Apart from Luftwaffe losses sustained over the British Isles there were a considerable number of fatalities resulting from operational flying that occurred at or near German aerodromes in occupied Europe. Some men died whilst taking off, landing or returning from operational sorties over enemy territory. Others, like 19-year-old Arno Raths, died as the result of flying accidents over mainland Europe. Obgefr Raths was an air gunner on board a Heinkel 111 of 8./KG55 that was involved in a mid-air collision near Versailles with another Heinkel 111, an indirect casualty of the air campaign against Britain. This was his original grave marker at a military cemetery in France.

The slaughter of Dornier 17-Zs had been relentless during July and August 1940, and the month of August was seen out with the loss of at least four aircraft of this type either on British soil or immediately off-shore on the 31st of the month. On that date about fifteen aircraft of II./KG3 attacked RAF Hornchurch where considerable damage was caused. This aircraft of the 4th Staffel was hit by fighters on return from the target. With the aircraft disabled the pilot, Ofw Willi Lange, made a near perfect forced landing on the sands at Sandwich Flats, Kent, at low tide. The aircraft came to rest near the Princes Golf Club with the crew managing to set fire to the aircraft before they could be prevented from doing so. This image of the swastika bedecked tailfin was later used as the basis for the design of one of the 25th anniversary Battle of Britain stamps issued by the Post Office in 1965. This caused some controversy in that a swastika appeared on a British stamp adjacent to the Queen's head.

All four of the crew were reported to be wounded on capture, although it is clear from this image that at least two of them can only have had fairly minor or superficial wounds. Here, Ofw Willi Lange takes up the rear as he and Fw Hans Wünsch are marched from the Golf Club building where they had been taken. They are about to be put into Army trucks as they begin their journey into some five years of captivity.

Chapter Four

The Battle's Crescendo: September 1940

Also raiding RAF Hornchurch on 31 August 1940 were the Dornier 17-Zs of 2./KG76 and one of these attackers was making its way home between Canterbury and Maidstone when it was set upon by about eight fighters which hit and disabled one engine and wounded three of the crew. Eventually, the aircraft made a crash landing at Newchurch on Kent's Romney Marsh and was badly damaged. In the RAF Intelligence Report it was noted that the aircraft carried an emblem that was: '... a shield of a bomb falling on a British lion'. Here is an example of the very same emblem to which that report refers, seen in this photograph on another of 2./KG76's Dornier 17-Z aircraft prior to taking off on a sortie over England.

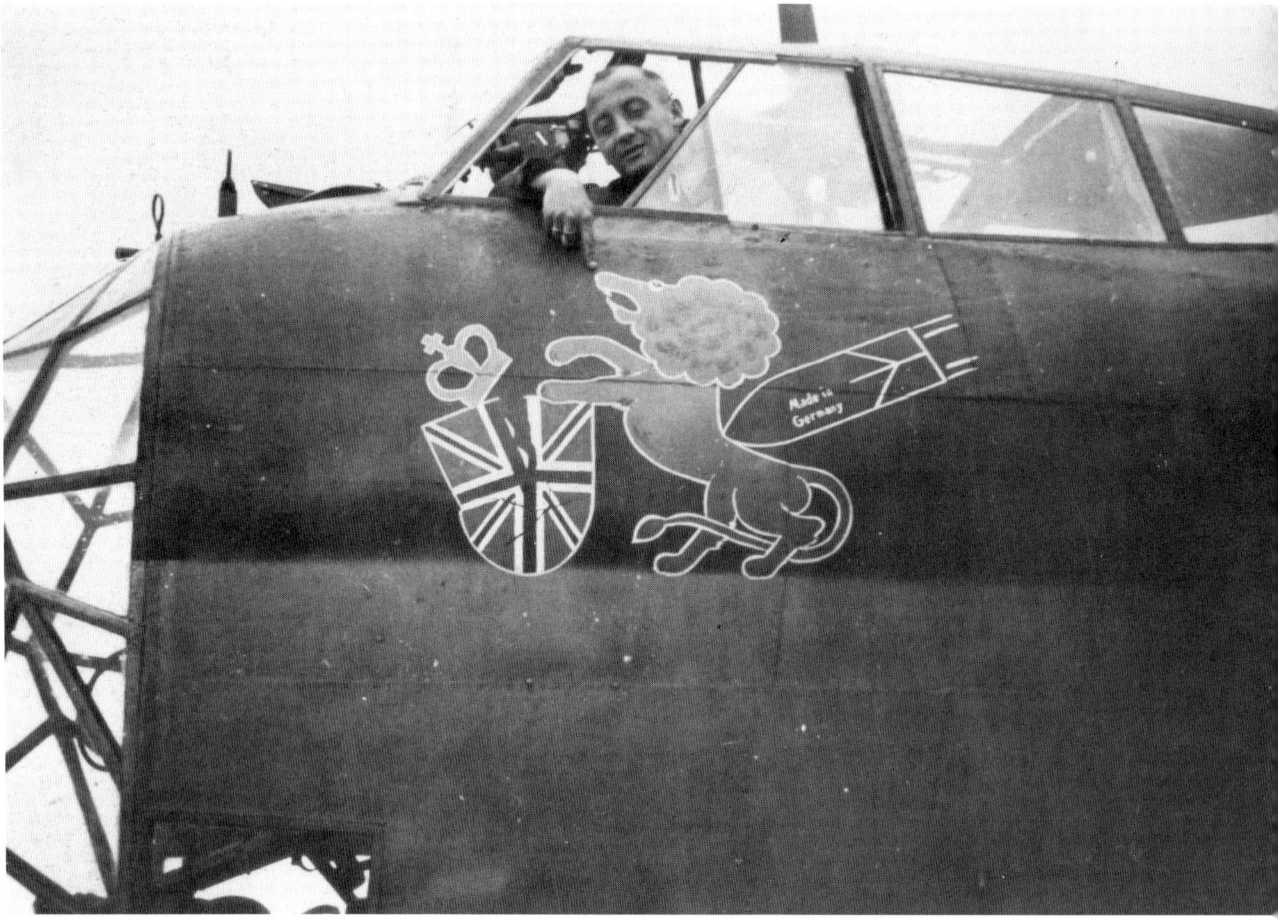
Made in Germany

For the first few days of September 1940 there were no losses of Luftwaffe bombers on land in the British Isles, although those days saw considerable fighter activity and losses involving both Messerschmitt 109s and 110s. Given that the majority of those losses were sustained as the fighters flew close-escort to bomber formations, one might conclude that the fighters were doing their job and preventing RAF fighters from getting through to the bombers. The first loss of a German bomber over Britain during the month of September was a Heinkel 111 of Stab I./KG1 shot down shortly after one o'clock in the morning at Rendlesham, Suffolk, on 5 September 1940. The aircraft had been on a night sortie to attack Tilbury Docks, but had been illuminated by searchlights and was then attacked by a Blenheim of 25 Squadron. On board the bomber had been the Gruppenkommandeur of I./KG1, Major Ludwig Maier, who was killed. Also killed were Ofw Erwin Stockert, Uffz Horst Bendig and Oblt Job-Wilhelm Graf von Rittberg. The pilot, Oblt Hans-Dietrich Biebrach, had a miraculous escape when he baled out at just 650ft. Not only had the Luftwaffe lost a high-ranking group commander, but two other relatively senior officers, both Oberleutnants, had been lost in what was almost certainly a very experienced crew. Clearly, the Luftwaffe bomber force was gearing up for its night offensive and the Blitz, evidence of this new phase not only being in the night target at Tilbury but also the fact that the aircraft had been daubed with lamp-black on its undersides and across the white of the fuselage crosses and tail swastikas.

(*Above*) The next night, sometime just after eleven o'clock, another Heinkel 111 night-bomber, this time from 6./KG4, took a direct hit from anti-aircraft fire, crashed and caught fire onto Suffolk Street, Sunderland. All four of the crew were killed, and there were civilian casualties on the ground. A Mrs Rachel Stormont, of 55 Suffolk Street, died. From a document found in the wreckage it was deduced that the target was probably Newcastle. The loss of two Heinkel 111 bombers on 5 September 1940, both of them at night time, started to paint a picture as to the direction in which the Luftwaffe bomber offensive against Britain was now heading. Indeed, 5 September 1940 was the very eve upon which the night Blitz against London and other cities would commence, although there would still be another two months of significant daylight activity by the enemy.

(*Opposite page*) By 7 September 1940 the day and night Blitz was getting into its stride. Night was a fairly effective defence for the Luftwaffe bomber force because at this stage of the war the RAF had had little experience of night fighting. Most interceptions took place when pilots picked out the enemy by sight alone. Airborne radar was only in its infancy and whilst anti-aircraft guns did pick off some victims it was certainly the case that darkness was the raider's friend. Daylight losses, though, continued as before and although the target emphasis had changed the Luftwaffe still continued to attack airfields, albeit not so intensely.

On 9 September, a POW from a 3./KG1 Heinkel 111 reported that the whole of I./KG1 (1, 2 & 3 Staffeln) had taken part in a raid against 'an aerodrome near London'. The prisoner in question was captured from this aircraft that had been shot down at Sundridge, near Sevenoaks, and in which all five crew were taken prisoner, two of them wounded. The Heinkel had been subjected to an attack by a Hurricane of 607 Squadron in which the bomber had been liberally sprayed with bullets, holes being found in both wings, engines, propellers and also on the port upper fuselage and starboard side of the nose. One engine had been stopped, the on-board intercom knocked out of action and in the crash landing the starboard wing had been badly smashed. Under the circumstances, the crew had had a lucky escape.

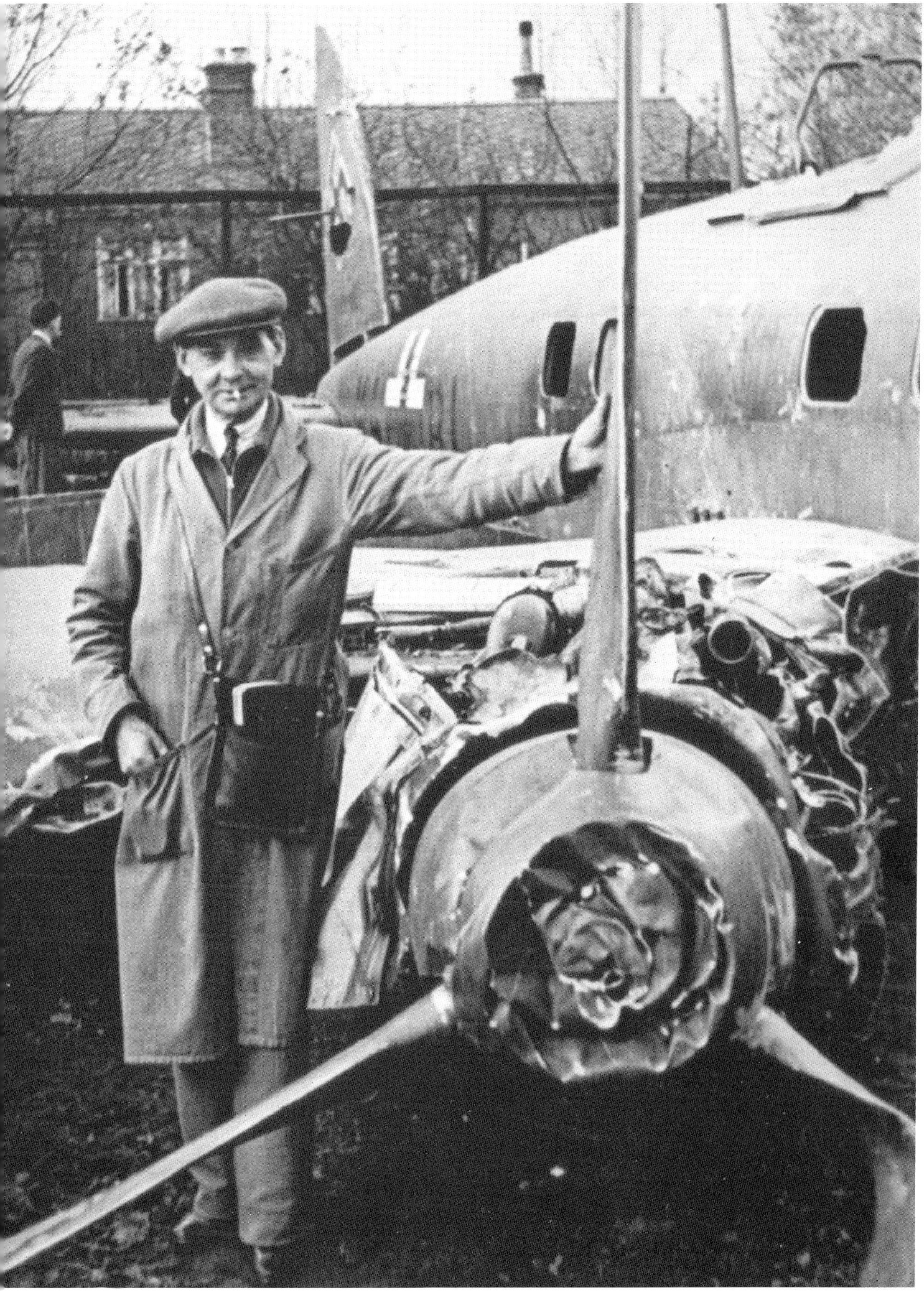

(*Above*) On 9 September 1940 a heavy raid was made against the London dockland area during late afternoon. One of those raiders was attacked by fighters, during which the starboard engine was hit and both radiators holed. With damage such as this there could be no hope of making it back across the English Channel, but it is believed that the pilot was trying to make for the Channel in hope of rescue by the efficient German air sea rescue service. This determination was possibly driven by the fact that on board was the Gruppenkommandeur of III./KG30, Major Wilhelm Hackbarth, son-in-law to Generalfeldmarschall Albert Kesselring who was the senior officer commanding the Air Fleet (Luftflotte 2) of which III./KG30 was a component part. In the event, with both propellers feathered and two of the crew members already dead from wounds, the pilot had no choice but to make a forced landing on the foreshore at Pagham Harbour, West Sussex. So much altitude had been lost that the Junkers 88 could not even stagger just a few more miles further out into the English Channel. In any case, Major Hackbarth had been very seriously wounded and was perhaps unlikely to survive a ditching at sea. The aircraft was extensively photographed by local photographer Frank Lalouette of Bognor Regis and this is the series of pictures he took, starting with a photograph of a soldier pointing out some of the fatal bullet holes in the bomber's nose glazing.

(*Opposite above*) A view of the bomber from the rear, showing a single white stripe underneath the swastika with the date 2.9.40 denoting an RAF fighter the crew had claimed to have shot down on that day.

(*Opposite below*) When originally published, this photograph was captioned 'Wrecking the Wreckers'. It shows soldiers who have just removed the swastika from the tail fin as a trophy.

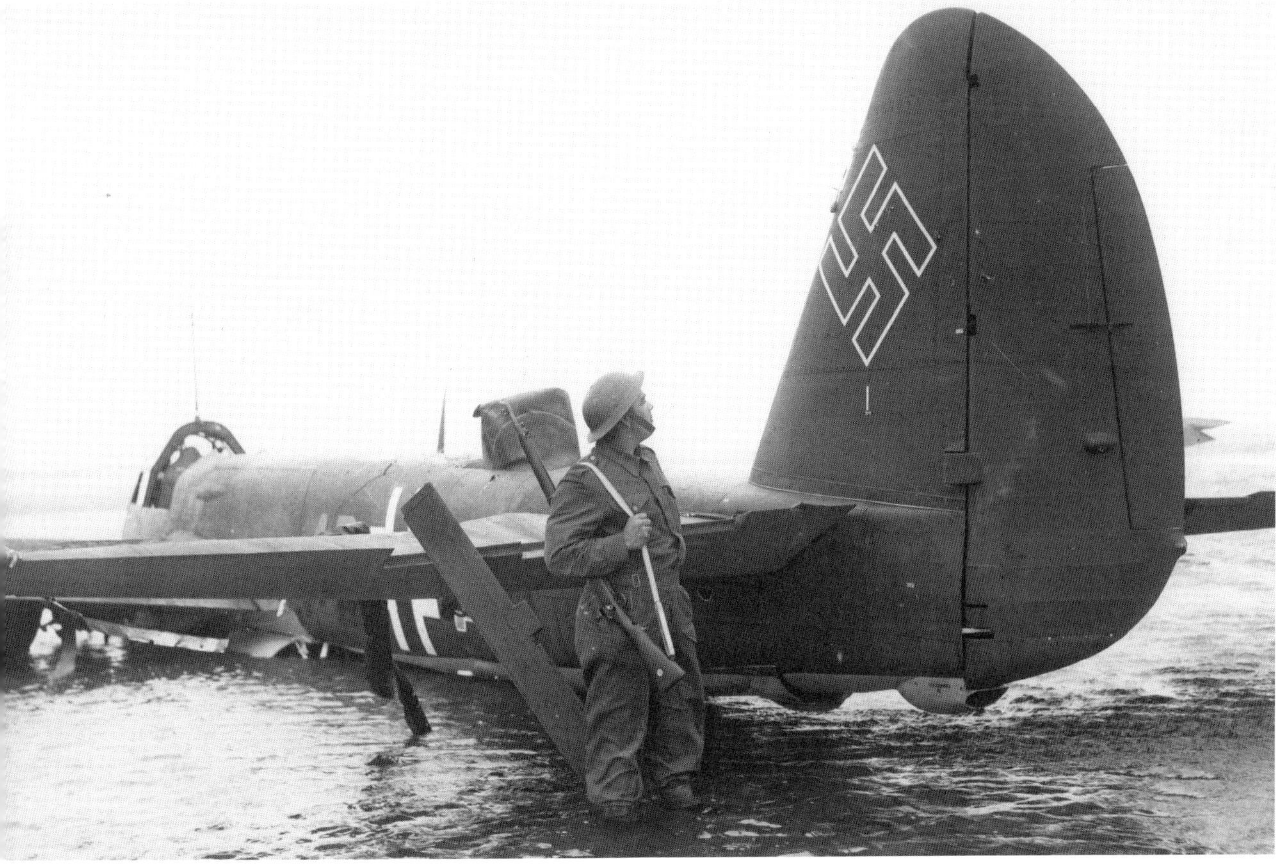

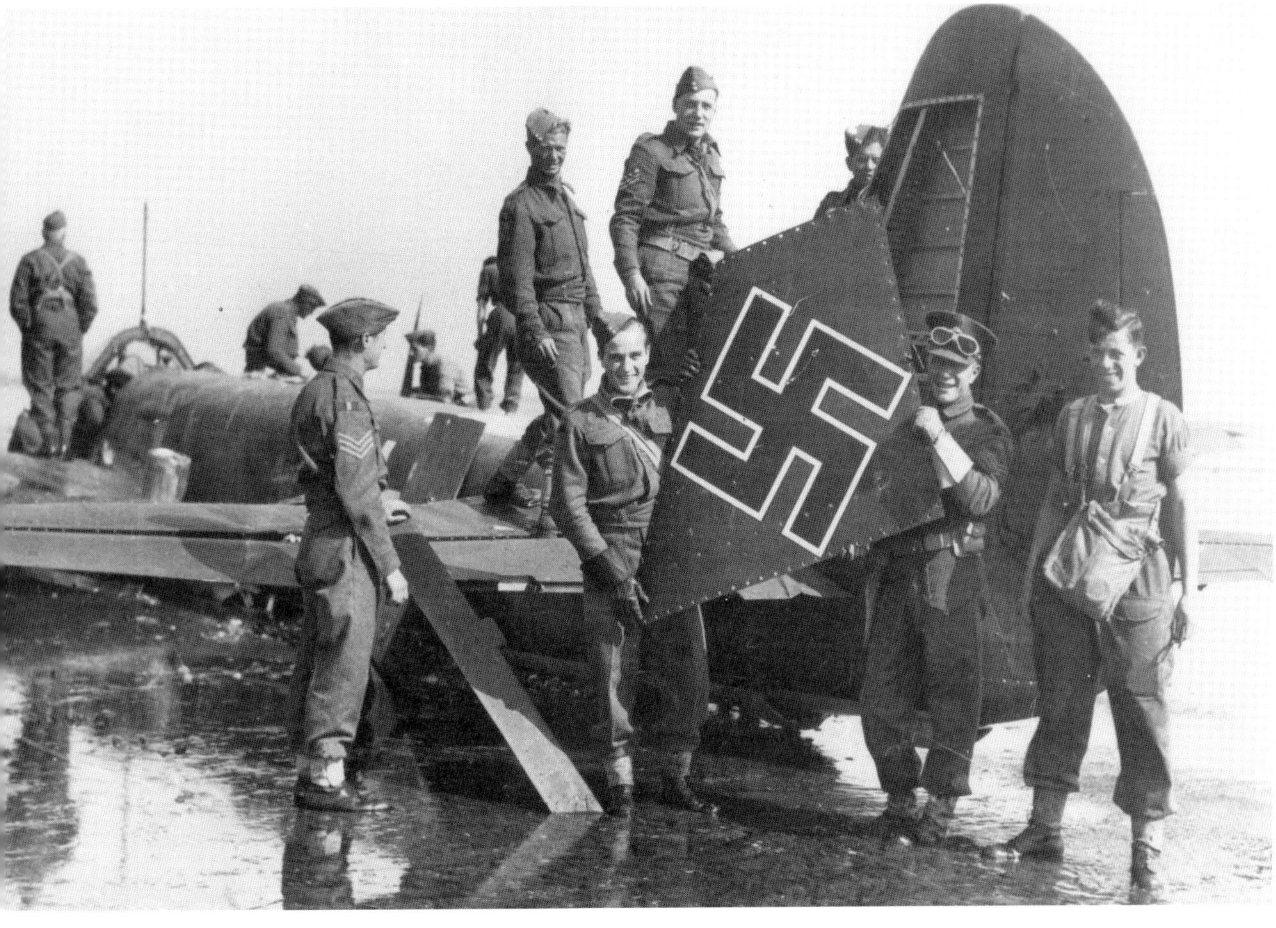

(*Above*) A Spaniel dog belonging to the soldiers guarding the wreck has contemptuously padded his paw prints across the wing as he surveys the scene.

(*Right*) Among the casualties on board was Gefr Friedrich Petermann, killed during the fighter attack just three days after his 21st birthday.

Another of the fatalities was Uffz Willi Sawallisch, photographed here on a stretcher by Frank Lalouette before his body was taken away. Lalouette placed this photograph on display in his shop window at Bognor Regis where it caused some public disquiet; he was eventually asked to take it down.

(*Above*) Major Hackbarth, seated front centre with walking stick, is seen here at Prisoner of War Camp No.23 that was situated at Kingwood near Godalming in Surrey. With him in this 1942 photograph are other captured Luftwaffe officer aircrew, all taken prisoner during 1940. Not all were bomber crew members, some were fighter pilots. They are, back row left to right and with date of capture and unit bracketed: Lt H.-G. Mollenbrok (16.8.40, 3./KG2), Oblt W. Blüme (18.8.40, 7./JG26), Maj W. Kienzle (30.9.40, Stab./JG26), Lt M. Himmelheber (6.9.40, Stab./JG2), Oblt C. Treiber (27.9.40, Stab II./JG52); front row, left to right: Oblt K. Welte (11.8.40, Stab.II/KG54), Hptm R. Bäss (30.8.40, 5./KG1), Maj J. Hackbarth (9.9.1940, Stab.III/KG30) Noster (no further details), Sonderführer A. Nothelfer (12.8.40, Stab/KG51). Several of these officers are linked to incidents that feature in some of the photographs elsewhere in this book.

(*Opposite above*) Wednesday 11 September 1940 was another bad day for the Heinkel 111s of KG1 with two of their aircraft being shot down and having to make forced landings on Broomhill Farm at East Guldeford, in East Sussex, within moments of each other. Both crews got out of their aircraft and set fire to them. A civilian on the outskirts of nearby Rye recorded the two distant funeral pyres on his Brownie Box Camera as the Heinkels were incinerated. Both aircraft had been on a sortie to bomb the London Docks.

(*Opposite below*) Close-up, and another photographer took this dramatic shot of one of the two Heinkels after the crew had torched it. All ten crew members from both bombers were taken prisoner by The Royal Irish Fusiliers.

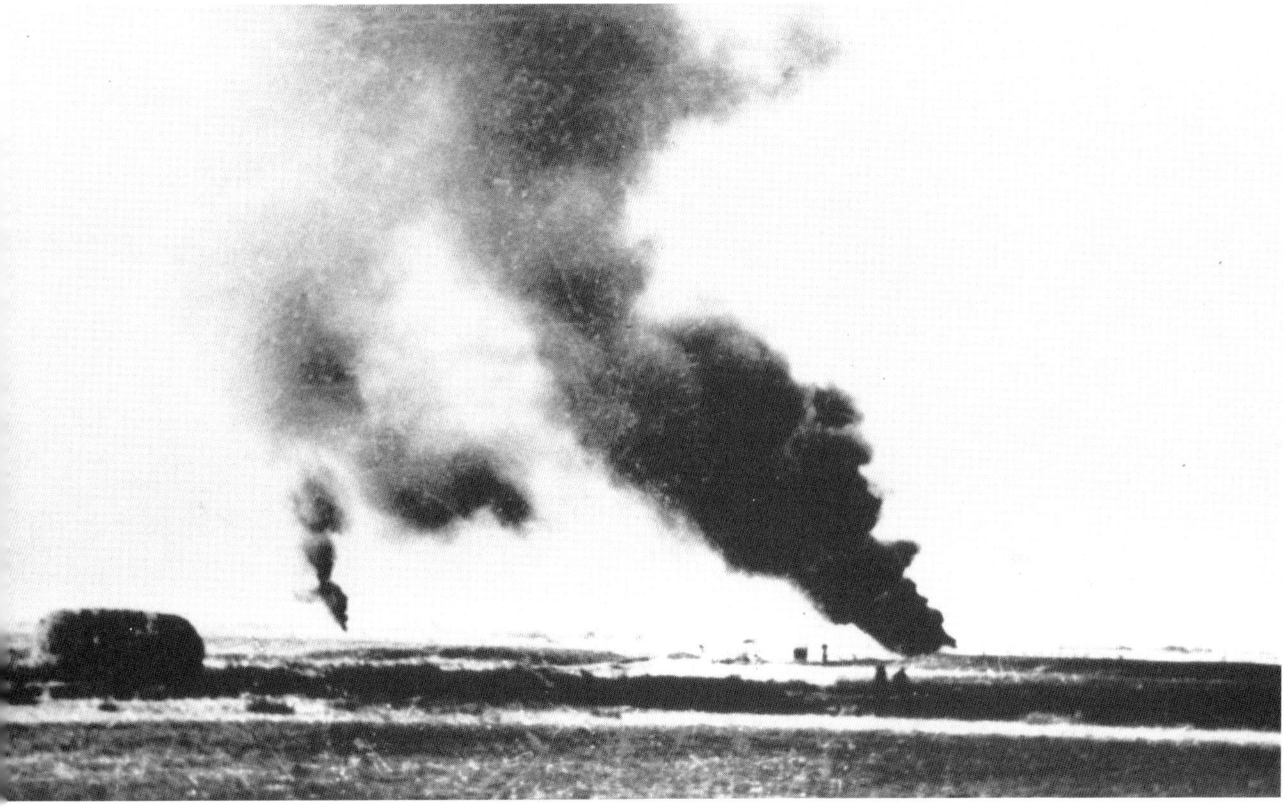

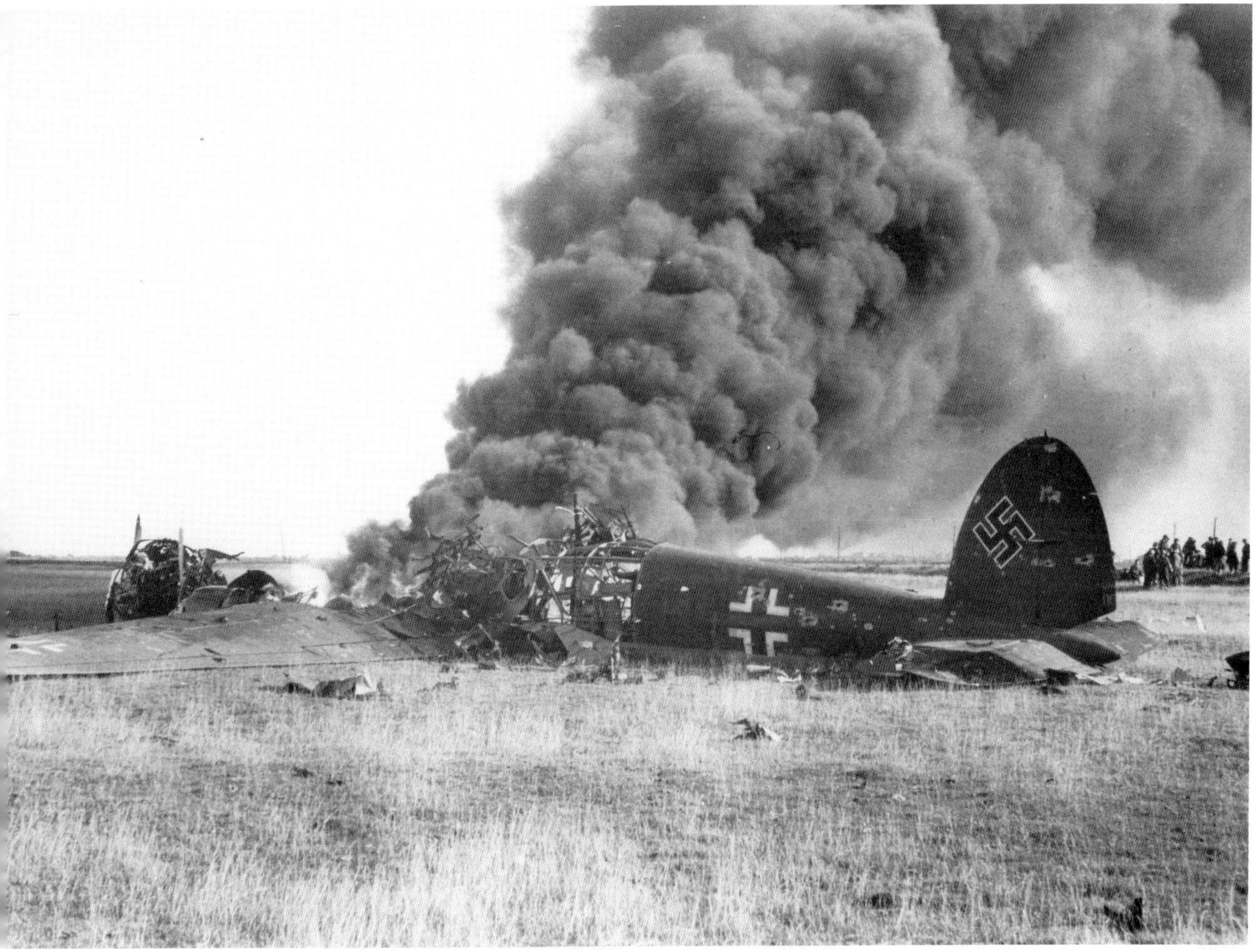

(*Above*) 'For you, the war is over!' Fw Heinz Friedrich manages a faint smile for the camera as he sits smoking a cigarette in an English field surrounded by his British captors. Meanwhile, another crew member (an Unteroffizier standing at top left) seems to be removing his watch at bayonet point. The two airmen were part of a five man crew of a He 111 of I./KG26 shot down at Burmash, Kent, on 11 September 1940. All five were taken POW.

(*Opposite above*) Sunday, 15 September 1940 is still marked as 'Battle of Britain Day' although it was certainly not the hardest fought day of the battle. That day was 18 August, 1940. However, 15 September did see some dramatic action above central London at around midday when a force of Dornier 17-Z bombers was intercepted by a mass of RAF fighters over the capital. One of the Dorniers from 1./KG76 was shot down above Victoria and had also been involved in a mid-air collision with a Hurricane of 504 Squadron flown by Sgt R.T. Holmes who baled out safely. The Dornier plummeted earthwards, disintegrating as it fell. Here, it is seen just a second or so away from final impact, pictured above the London skyline and already minus its outboard wing sections and tail as it begins to break up. Two of the crew lost their lives in this incident, and the Dornier slammed onto the forecourt of Victoria Station demolishing James Walker's clock shop.

(*Opposite below*) Firemen hose down the wreckage of the shop and the blazing Dornier. Mercifully, there were no casualties on the ground. As it was a Sunday there was nobody in the shop, and the relatively few people who might have been around had probably taken cover due to the fact that an air raid warning had been sounded.

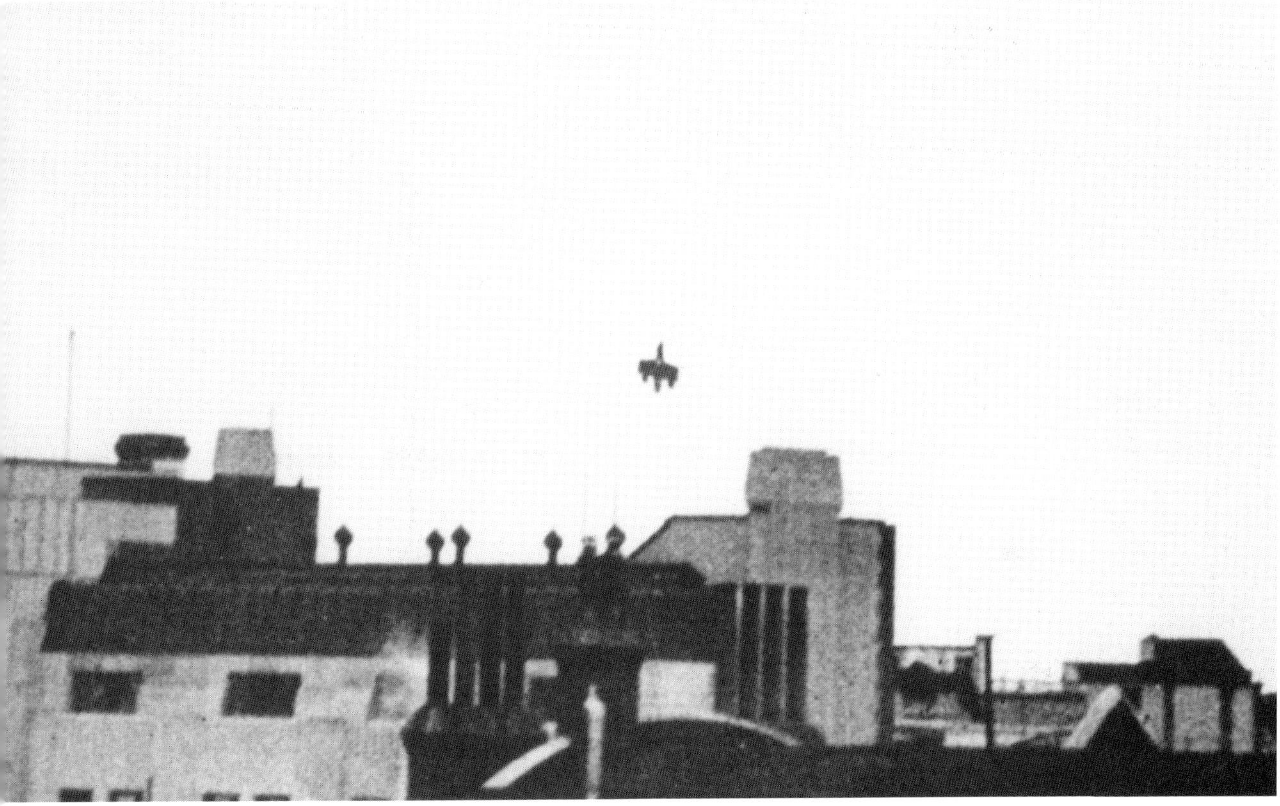

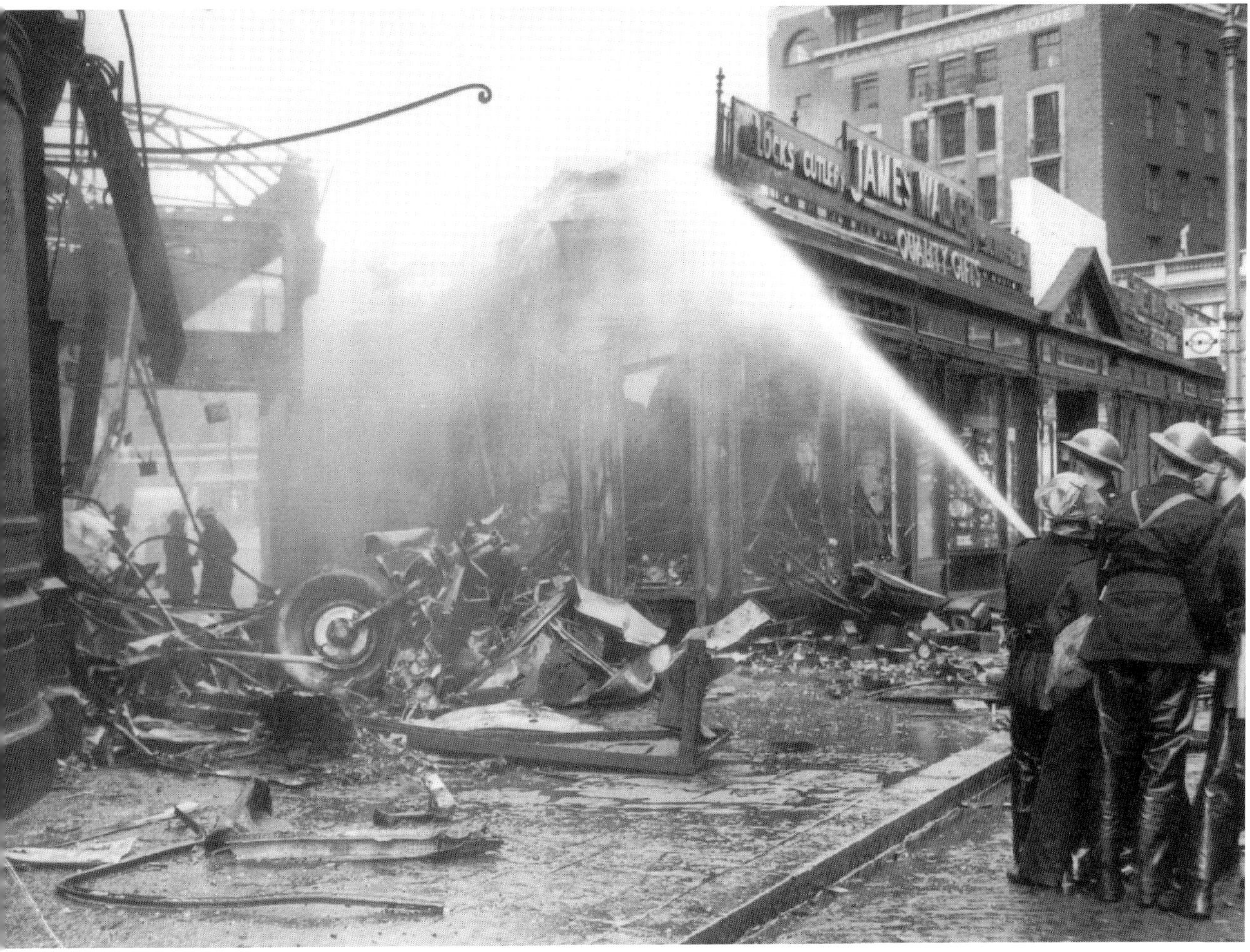
LOCKS
JAMES
QUALITY GIFTS

(*Above*) With the fire extinguished, two police officers examine an engine and propeller partially buried in the pavement. Scars to the façade of the station (the building visible behind the policemen) are still extant more than seventy years later. A scatter of James Walker's famed mantel clocks litter the pavement amongst a sea of shattered plate glass from the shop window and myriad bits of mangled Dornier.

(*Right*) Although his damaged Heinkel 111 got back to its home base on 15 September 1940, Uffz Paul Schüll of 8./KG55 had been killed in a fighter attack over Portland in Dorset and was buried here in this French cemetery by his comrades.

To the casual observer, this looks to be nothing more than a woodland pond. In fact, it is the crater blasted by an exploding Dornier 17-Z of 5./KG3 when shot down on 15 September 1940 into Combwell Wood, Kilndown, right on the Kent/Sussex border. The bomb load of the Dornier detonated some while after impact, killing Volunteer William Waters of the 23rd (Hawkhurst) Btn, Home Guard. If one knows where to look, the fingerprints of war, left behind by the Battle of Britain, are still to be seen.

(*Above*) A raider that managed to limp back to France on 15 September and eventually crashed near Poix was this bullet-riddled Dornier 17-Z of I./KG76. Its pilot, Uffz Hans Figge, had nursed it back across the English Chanel with over 200 bullet holes.

(*Right*) Not returning to France on 15 September 1940 was Oblt Peter Schierning of II./KG53, taken prisoner when he baled out of his Heinkel 111 above Frittenden in Kent. The aircraft had been damaged by anti-aircraft fire whilst bombing the Victoria Docks and was then set upon by Spitfires. Six men were in the crew, including Major M. Gruber the Gruppenkommandeur. Five of them survived, while one man, Fw Andreas Grassl, had been killed in the fighter attack.

Although the successes of Royal Artillery anti-aircraft batteries were generally somewhat limited, an exception to this rule was the claimed destruction of a Dornier 17-Z by 166 Battery of the 55th Heavy Anti Aircraft Regiment, RA, on 15 September 1940. However, and rather like the Heinkel shot down at Frittenden, it is more likely that in this instance they were a contributing factor rather the direct cause of the bomber's destruction. The aircraft, of 8./KG2, had been on a sortie to bomb the London docks when it was attacked first by a Hurricane of 253 Squadron and then a Spitfire of 66 Squadron, as well as being engaged by the heavy guns of 166 Battery and so it is likely that all three played a part in its demise. Ultimately, and after all four of the crew had abandoned the doomed aircraft, it crashed onto a house at 13 The Chase, Chatham, Kent, shortly after three o'clock in the afternoon. Later, the men from 166 Battery were photographed with a swastika bedecked tail fin taken from the wreck of the Dornier as they posed in front of one of the battery guns. It was very often the case that German bombers were 'winged' by AA fire, only to be finished off in a *coup-de-grace* by fighter aircraft.

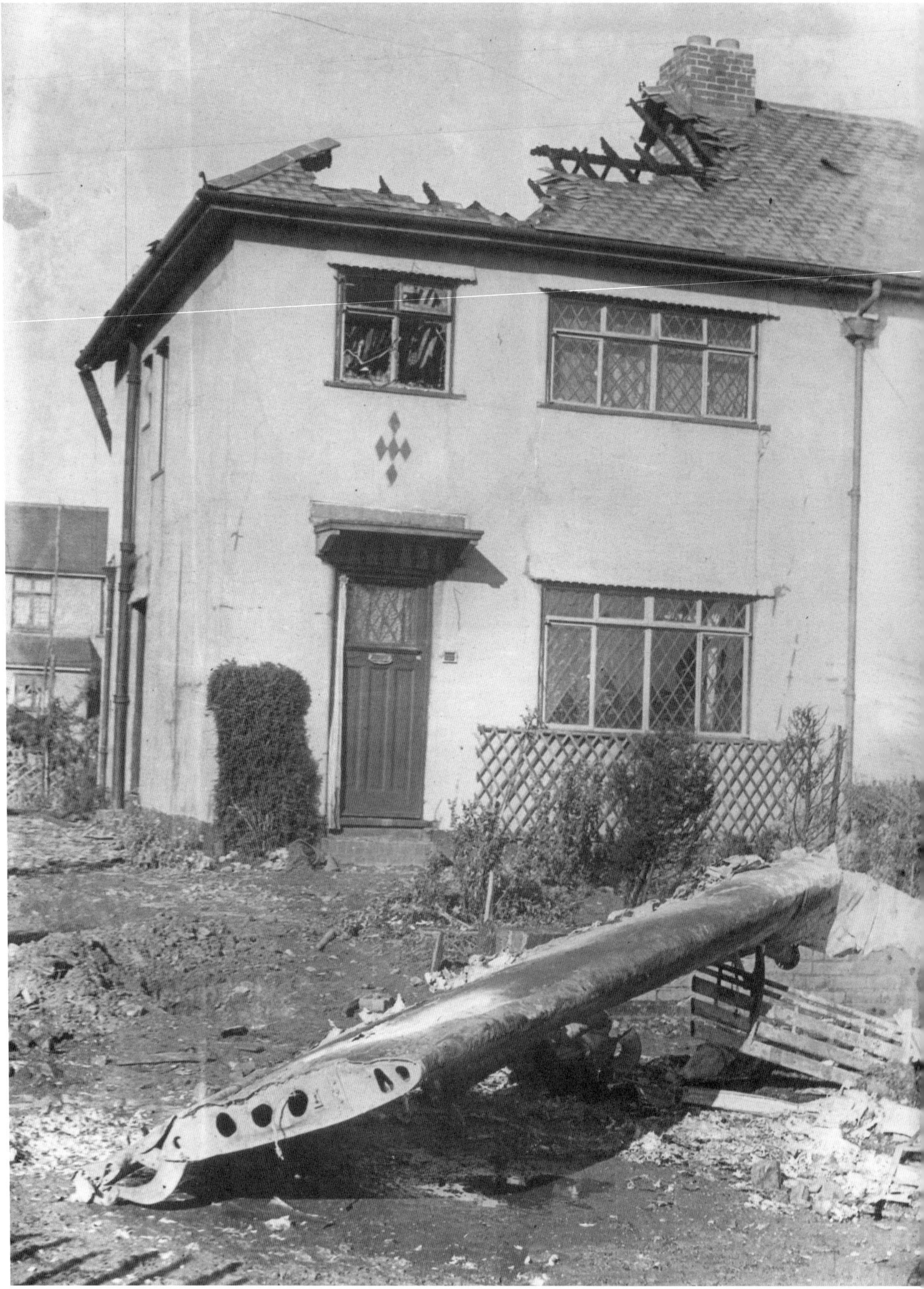

(*Above*) Sometimes Luftwaffe losses over Britain were rather less eventful and came about through no cause of the defending forces. On 19 September 1940 a Junkers 88 of 4.(F)/121, a reconnaissance unit, was undertaking a photo-recce sortie when it developed a mechanical problem in the port engine. The sight of RAF fighters nearby made the crew conclude that they could not escape, and they made a wheels-up landing at RAF Oakington in Cambridgeshire. All four crew members were captured unhurt and the aircraft was later dismantled and despatched to the Royal Aircraft Establishment at Farnborough for examination. The unit emblem of 4.(F)/121, an owl perched on a pencil, can be seen in this photograph taken at Farnborough where three journalists can be seen trying the rather cramped cockpit for size and giving a good impression of how cramped it must have been in the confined cockpit for four men.

(*Opposite page*) Another enemy bomber that crashed onto a residential dwelling in Kent was this Junkers 88 of 3./ KG54, shot down on a night raid, again to the London Docks, on 17 September 1940. The aircraft was intercepted by an RAF Defiant night-fighter and sent crashing to earth at Maidstone, Kent, where the falling wreckage landed in St Andrew's Close and Tonbridge Road shortly before midnight. All four crew members were killed and the ARP Report later noted: 'Fire at six houses; two reported gutted and badly damaged. Also, one garage containing a private car adjoining St Andrews Close burnt out, plus eight other houses and a school in near vicinity with damaged roofs. One woman killed and another woman and a man slightly injured.' The dead woman was 67-year-old Rose Bridgeland, killed in her home at No. 1 St Andrew's Close, the injured man a Mr Frank Hook, and the woman a Mrs Pett of 2 St Andrew's Close. Sometimes, civilians and others on the ground paid a heavy price for the destruction of enemy raiders. This was the aftermath at Maidstone, with scorched debris from the Junkers 88 strewn around the garden of one of the burnt-out houses. Rescuers described the house as being 'surrounded by a ring of fire'.

(*Above*) Rather less intact was another Junkers 88 shot down the same day at Culford School, Bury St Edmunds, Suffolk. The aircraft, of 1./KG77, was shot down by Hurricanes of 302 (Polish) Squadron during a sortie to bomb London and crashed in flames, killing three of the crew. Only one man, Uffz Erich Etzold, survived to be taken into captivity.

(*Opposite page*) With the Luftwaffe bomber force being committed more and more to night operations, so any conspicuous light markings that might show up in the glare of a searchlight were obliterated with a black distemper paint or lampblack. This included the crude painting over of crosses and swastikas so as to cover up the white paint. Similarly, the light blue under-surfaces were often painted over with black. Here, two soldiers puzzle over the painted-out swastika on the tail of the Junkers 88 of 3./LG1 that had been shot down through the combined efforts of Hurricanes of 238 Squadron and Spitfires of 602 Squadron, as well as being shot at by anti-aircraft guns. The aircraft came to earth on Mudberry Farm at Bosham in West Sussex on 21 September 1940 and the *Sussex Gazette* carried a dramatic contemporary account of the episode. Unusually, it also gave the location of the crash: 'The German bomber was rocked by AA fire before two Spitfires pounced on its tail. The raider glided round in a semi-circle, eventually crashing at Bosham. It brushed the roof of the Nunnery and cleared the roof of a motor bus on the main road by inches, giving the passengers and driver the fright of their lives. It cleared a railway train by the same narrow margin and crashed in a meadow. Immediately it was surrounded by a swarm of thirty boys who had been blackberrying in the neighbouring fields. Without thought for the danger they jumped over electrified rails to meet the four Germans who clambered out of the machine. It fell close to the railway, having collided with telegraph wires.'

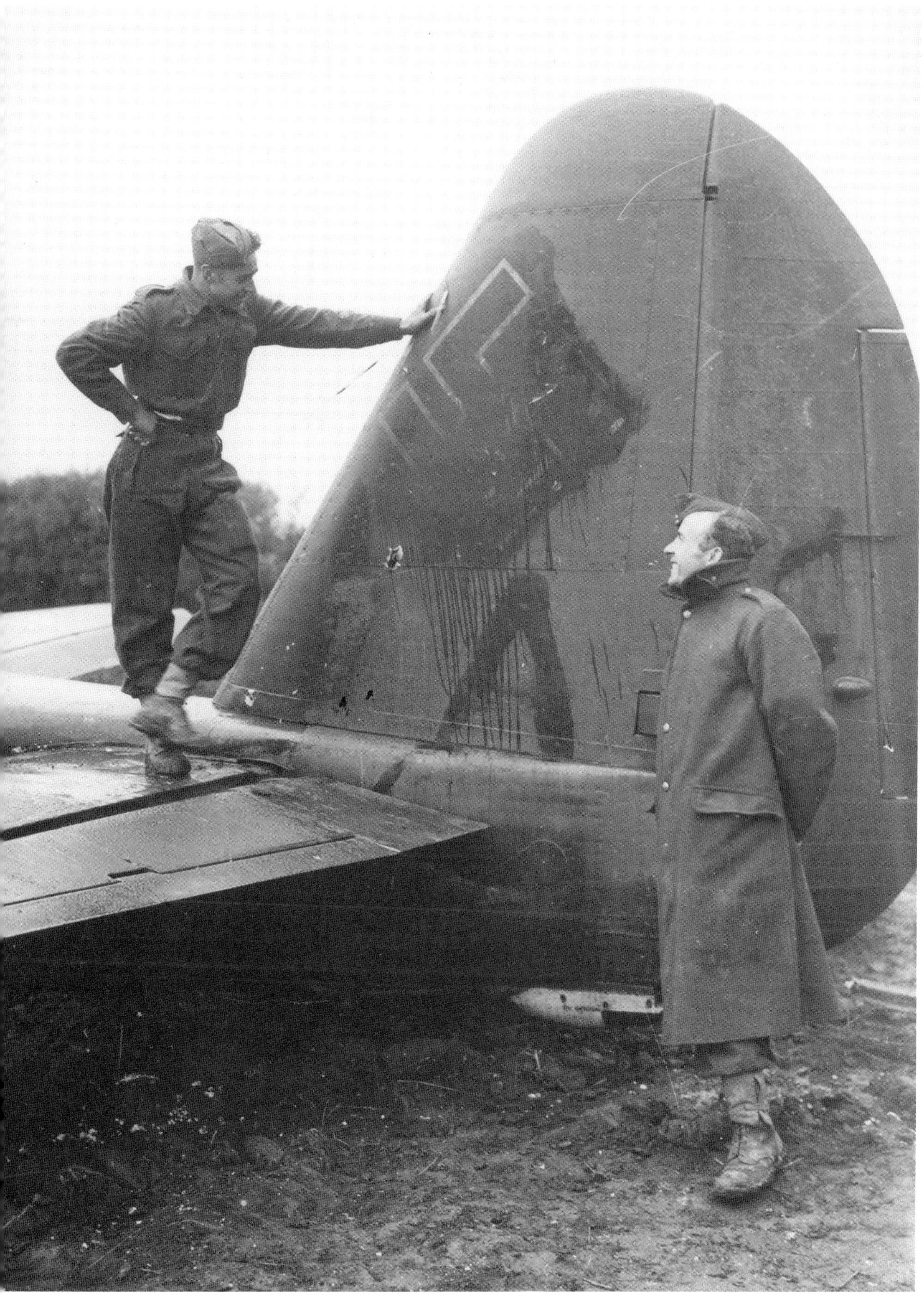

(*Above*) A general view of the crashed Junkers 88 with a soldier pointing to the impressive red dragon on a white shield beneath the cockpit. Beyond can be seen the course of the railway line, marked out by the telegraph poles, supporting the cables with which the Junkers 88 collided. On impact, both propeller assemblies have been torn from the engines.

(*Right*) On 27 September 1940 in the west of England, the Messerschmitt 110-D aircraft of Erprobungsgruppe 210 had been back in action (see page 41), this time detailed to attack the Parnall Aircraft Works at Yate. One of the aircraft was shot down by Hurricanes of 504 Squadron, being forced to make a forced landing at The Beeches, Iwerne Minster. Although the pilot was captured unhurt, his radio operator/air gunner, 20-year-old Gefr Werner Zwick, was very badly wounded. So serious were his wounds that he was among the group of Luftwaffe aircrew personnel repatriated on medical grounds in a reciprocal arrangement with the Germans for the release of similarly injured British POWs. The exchange was organised via the International Red Cross in 1943.

Enemy aircraft that were actually destroyed by anti-aircraft fire were relatively few in number, but a Heinkel 111 of 5./ KG55 that was taking part in a raid on the Bristol Aero Works was badly damaged to the extent that the five crew were forced to abandon the aircraft, leaving it to crash and break up on impact at Racecourse Farm, Portbury, around midday on 27 September 1940. A chunk of wing, with undercarriage attached, provides shelter for two soldiers and their terrier dog as they take refreshment. The aircraft spread itself in pieces across three large fields.

It has often been called 'The Battle of Graveney Marshes', and is sometimes billed as the first engagement between enemy forces on British soil since the Battle of Fishguard in 1797. The truth was very much removed from what has grown up as something of a myth of the Battle of Britain. On 27 September 1940, at about three-forty in the afternoon, this Junkers 88 of 3./KG77 made what was, by now, a singularly unremarkable arrival in a forced landing on Graveney Marshes, close to The Sportsman Inn, near Faversham. A party of the London Irish Regiment rushed across the open fields to capture the crew, but then fired on the German airmen as they left the aircraft. It was reported that shots were exchanged between the Germans and the British soldiers, with some versions of the tale having the Germans holding out for hours and even taking over a sandbagged gun emplacement. It is thought that the German crew *may* have fired at the aircraft in efforts to destroy it, and it is certainly a fact that they were fired at by the London Irish Regiment soldiers with one crew member, Uffz Ruhlandt, being shot through the ankle. Further to this part of the story, a Captain Cantopher of the London Irish Regiment was awarded the George Medal for dashing to the aircraft and removing a timed destruction device before throwing it into a nearby drainage ditch. But beyond this, the stories are almost certainly rather more than fanciful. This photograph shows the nose section of the Junkers 88 at Graveney Marsh on 27 September, bearing the heraldic emblem of KG77 and the name 'Eule' (Owl).

(*Left*) Uffz Fritz Ruhlandt was the pilot of the Graveney Marshes Junkers 88. He avoided giving any specific detail of the circumstances of his capture on 27 September 1940 when contacted by the author in 1987.

(*Right*) Rather more forthcoming about the events that day was the radio operator/air gunner, Uffz Erwin Richter. Writing in 1987 he said: 'During an anti-aircraft engagement over London one engine failed. As a result we were separated from our unit formation and were immediately attacked by three fighters. Ruhlandt dived at once, and as he neared the ground he found that the second engine had failed as the result of fighter fire. There was no longer any opportunity to get out, as we were so near the ground. So, we had to make an emergency landing. During the fighter attack I was wounded in both eyes by glass splinters. Uffz Ruhlandt was wounded by a shot through the ankle on the ground. The other two crew members remained unharmed. A detachment of soldiers arrested us and took us into custody, where we were very well treated. After interrogation I was taken to a hospital and operated on in both eyes.' Neither Ruhlandt nor Richter mentioned anything of the supposed 'battle' or 'skirmish' and it seems likely that if anything did happen then it was simply the crew firing at the aircraft trying to destroy it, with the London Irish then firing shots to dissuade them from doing so, and hitting Uffz Ruhlandt. Quite possibly the tale about the 'battle' was born in The Sportsman Inn that night over several pints of Guinness. It has certainly been elaborated and embroidered ever since then, to the point where fiction has almost become an established historical fact.

Chapter Five

Autumnal Changes:
October 1940

Although we have commented on the successes or otherwise of British anti-aircraft fire in countering Luftwaffe raiders, October 1940 saw a different turn of events with several losses due entirely to both light and heavy AA guns. This Junkers 88 of Stab I./KG77 succumbed to ground fire from light machine guns and 40mm Bofors guns during a bombing attack on the de Havilland Aircraft Works at Hatfield aerodrome at around half past eleven on the morning of Thursday, 3 October 1940. The aircraft crashed in flames on Eastend Green Farm, Hertingfordbury. The four crew members had all managed to escape the aircraft before it was almost completely engulfed in flames.

On 8 October 1940 three Heinkel 111s of 8./KG55 took part in a low-level attack across West Sussex and Hampshire, but somewhere north of Chichester they were engaged by anti-aircraft guns, the fire hitting one of the Heinkels and sending it exploding into the grounds of Stansted House, Stoughton, near Rowlands Castle. Such was the force of the explosion that only one crew member out of the five on board could be found and identified. He was the pilot, Fw Ernst Ens, who was buried at nearby RAF Thorney Island. Very little of the bomber was left for this Home Guardsmen to guard. An RAF pilot, Plt Off Gilbert Elliott, was killed on the ground when he rushed from Stansted House, where he was a guest, to see if anyone was trapped alive in the wreckage. As he did so, he was hit by machine bullets from the exploding wreckage and died later in hospital.

(*Left*) Gefr Hans Pawlik, a former fruit and vegetable barrow-boy from a rural German village, was one of the crew from the Heinkel 111 and was its wireless operator/air gunner. He took off that day with a foreboding premonition. No trace of him was ever found.

(*Right*) Lt Ulrich Flugge was the observer on board the ill-fated Heinkel that day. This earlier photograph of him was taken when he held the rank of NCO.

(*Below*) This Luftwaffe belt buckle was picked up in the wreckage and kept as a souvenir by PC Sid Reynolds who was involved with the Magistrates Court case mentioned on page 28. This item had probably belonged to Fw Ernst Ens.

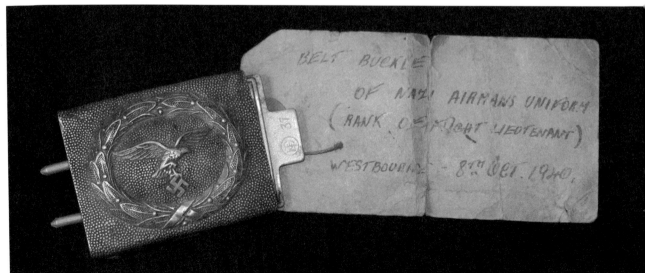

Despite the almost total disintegration of the bomber, RAF Intelligence Officers investigating the wreck found the remains of the rudder with an emblem of three red fishes on a yellow shield. Here, the same emblem is seen on the rudder of another 8./KG55 machine.

On 10 October 1940, at half past four in the morning, this Junkers 88 plunged into the River Roach in Essex at Horseshoe Corner, Foulness Island. All of the crew baled out into captivity over Stanford-le-Hope, Essex, after the 8./KG51 aircraft had been hit by anti-aircraft fire during an attack on London's East India Docks. This photograph was taken of the aircraft, numbered 0299 and bearing the code letters 9K+HS, shortly before it took off on its fateful sortie over England. It would appear that the anti-aircraft defences were 'getting their eye-in' and apparently becoming more efficient.

(*Above*) By 24 October 1940, when this photograph was taken, daylight raiders over the British Isles being shot down by RAF fighters were becoming something of a rarity. In fact, this was also quite a rare aircraft type to be downed over Britain. It is a Dornier 215-B that was flying a daylight photo reconnaissance mission to Coventry with the Luftwaffe unit 3./Aufkl.Gr.Ob.d.L. It was intercepted by three Hurricanes of 1 Squadron and sent into the ground at Eaton Scocon, Bedfordshire, where it crashed into a field behind The Crown Inn. Only one man survived, although he was badly injured. The other three crew members baled out too low for their parachutes to open and were killed.

(*Opposite above*) Another October victim of ground fire. This Junkers 88 of 7./KG4 was brought down by ground fire during a low-level attack on RAF Linton-on-Ouse. Three of the crew were captured unhurt when the aircraft crashed on Richmond Farm at Duggleby in Yorkshire at around six o'clock in the evening. One crew member, Uffz O. Piontek, was very severely wounded and died of his injuries on 15 November 1940. The Staffel emblem of a bat over a moon is pointed out by a lance-corporal for the benefit of the press photographer.

(*Opposite below*) On board the Duggleby Junkers 88 aircraft was Oblt Friedrich Podblieski, Staffelkapitän of the 7th Staffel of KG4. He is seen here relaxing before a sortie and is sitting on the right in his flying overalls in front of one of the unit's Junkers 88 aircraft.

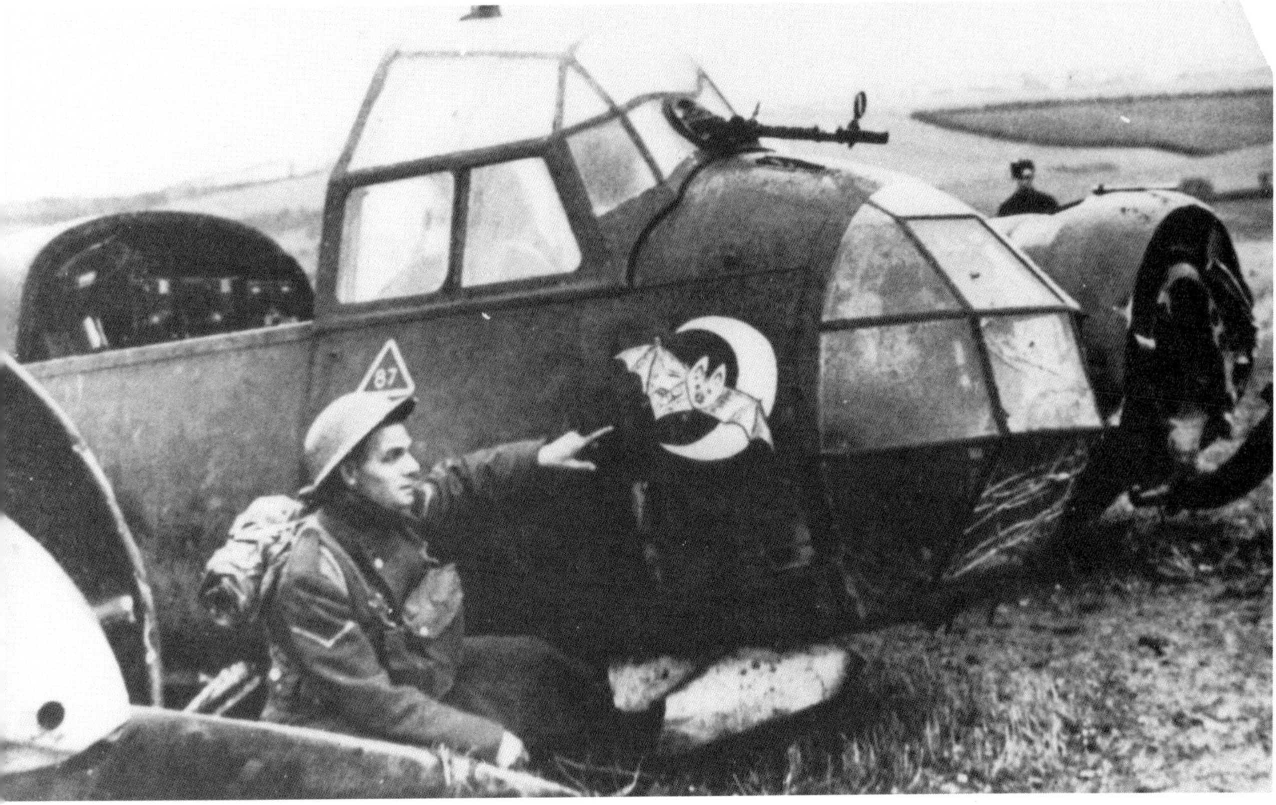
87

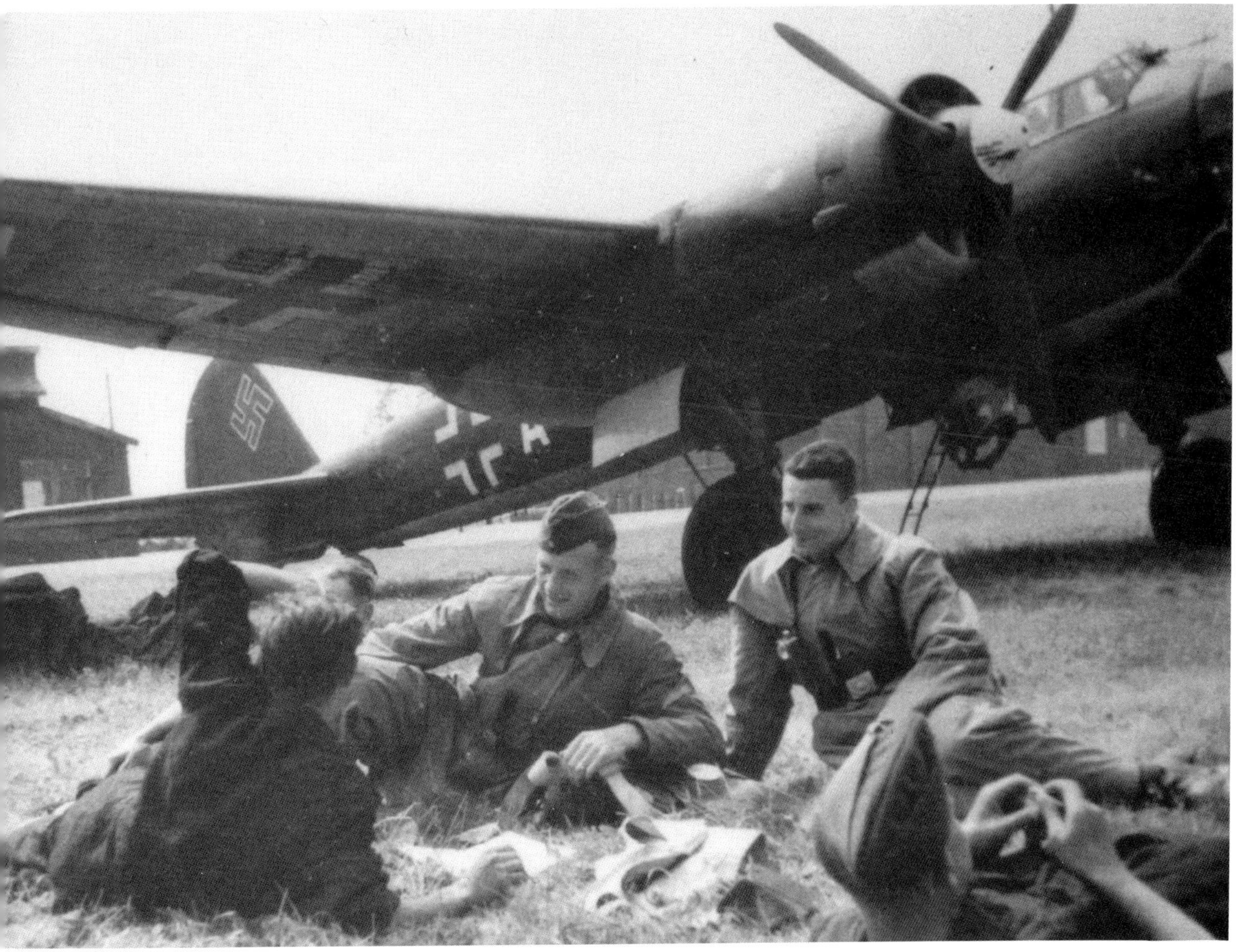

The Luftwaffe air campaign against the British Isles is perhaps epitomised in this iconic image of a Heinkel 111 photographed during the Battle of Britain, high above the distinctive curves of the River Thames through East London and directly over Wapping on 7 September 1940 at around quarter to six in the afternoon. Generally, 7 September is thought of as the first day of the Blitz. So often, the area seen in this image would be at the receiving end of the German bombers unwelcome attention. Although the Battle of Britain officially came to an end on 31 October 1940 there would yet be many months of the Blitz to be endured by civilians, defenders and attackers.

Notes

Notes